Vocabulous Throwdown™

Now Entering: The Word Zone

Volume 2

By:
Matt Quenville &
Sketchi Bill

With SketchiToons® by Sketch Bill

By permission of NExSW, Inc.

An  Production

AbVocab Publishing, Inc

Santa Fe, New Mexico

No part of this publication may be reproduced or transmitted in any form or by any means, electronic or mechanical, including photocopy, recording or any information storage or retrieval system, without permission in writing from the publisher.

ISBN-13 978-1-7353279-3-8

SketchiToons®in in frames are used by permission by Northeast by Southwest, Inc.
to create the derivative works in the picture frames contained within.
Original Copyright retained by Northeast by Southwest, Inc.

Other Frames include derivative works by Matt Quenville.

Attributions for SketchiToons® and other frames are given in a later section of the book.

Various Illustrations by Sketchi Bill

Cover Art by Sketchi Bill & Matt Quenville

Absolutely Vocabulous, Vocabulous Throwdown, Abvocab and Abvocab Publishing are trademarks of
AbVocab Publishing, Inc

SketchiToons®, Sketchi, Sketchi Bill are trademarks of Northeast by Southwest, Inc.

All other trademarks are the property of their respective companies.

Printing History:
July 2020
10 9 8 7 6 5 4 3 2 1

Table of Contents

Acknowledgements	4
Forward (Author's Note)	5
Brain-o-meter Levels	7
Quotes	8
PC Warning	9
Mains Words, Definitions & Art	10-79
Word Definitions	80-86
Related Words	87-91
Attributions	92-94
About	95

Author Acknowlegements

Matt Quenville acknowledges with pleasure the decent set of genes he received from his father Tom Quenville and mother Susan Quenville. Dad taught the importance of work ethic and mom encouraged the pursuit of this book and was always a champion of education. Both Tom & Sue raised their kids to think independently and not be boxed in by dogmatism and ideology. Also want to acknowledge the role happenstance plays in life. Tom introduced Matt to Sketchi Bill (Tom's old college roommate). This book is the result of that collaboration. Also, happenstance that this quarantine time would allow him to take time to pursue a creative piece of work that he would otherwise have not had the time to complete. Finally, would like to give a shout out to my kids Jordan and Ansley and wife Afton for support.

Sketchi Bill proudly acknowledges the wonderful lifetime cast of creative and fun-loving characters he has been fortunate enough to work and play with - and more importantly to learn from. In particular, from his earlier professional life Professor Charles Kruger and Mr. Vincent Moeyersoms. And especially, the exceptional human beings that are his kids, Chris and Jana, and his grandkids Rafa and Sandro. Great thanks to Barbara Hunter-Harmon who has critiqued many sketches and has provided an opportunity for spirited discussions about the widest variety of topics, keeping ideas flowing. Memories and thoughts from these folks and so many others are embedded in the sketches. Without them, Sketchi would never been even close to the line of sanity.

Author's Note

Why read this book? So here's the deal. You gotta take these tests in High School & College that supposedly measure your intelligence and what you have learned. After college, society will fork you over a bill that you will spend the rest of your life paying back, usually with interest. Before I became a teacher, I took these silly ass tests too. Whether or not you get into your favorite college or grad school will partly depend on your score on these tests. The least I can do is make it fun for you to learn stuff and do well on the tests. You'll master these words when you are done reading, fo' sho'. Maybe it will help you get a scholarship or accepted to your favorite college. Or just use the book for some shits & giggles & expand your vocabulary.

These entries include curse words and sexual references here and there because they reflect your life experiences & certainly future ones. If nothing else, all that fortnite & foodie shows and music videos & talking trash on Snapchat & Instagram has prepared you for this approach. This book is unlike any other vocabulary study book out there. It is an uncensored, uninhibited study guide written in your language, in your world, using your slang, ya' hurd.

Seriously, it is important that you do well on these tests. I've prepared much of this material myself, with an eye connecting to your world. This book was co-written by Sketchi Bill, an old, but irreverent and whimsical sort.

So, let's vocabulously throwdown. These tests are important. Enjoy the humor and learn the words.

With best luck,

Matt Quenville

Brain-o-Meter Word Levels

Brain-o-Meter Level 1

Softball word: slightly stimulating, brain still on cruise control

BOM 1

Brain-o-Meter Level 2

Moderately hard: get the juices flowing, stimulating but not much brain pain

BOM 2

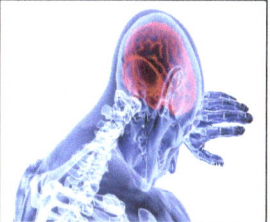

Brain-o-Meter Level 3

Wicked hard: neurons flying, brain is on fire

BOM 3

Brain-o-Meter Level 4

Damn, I can't even pronounce this. My mind is blown. Words of the Elite.

BOM 4

*Brain-o-meter from here on out will be abbreviated as BOM

Quotes

"Without freedom of thought, there can be no such thing as wisdom and no such thing a public liberty without freedom of speech" Ben Franklin

"The universe may have a purpose, but nothing we know suggests that, if so, this purpose has any similarity to ours" Bertrand Russell

"Your time is limited, so don't waste it living someone else's life. Don't be trapped by dogma- which is living with the results of other people's thinking. Don't let the noise of other's opinions drown out your own inner voice. And most important, have the courage to follow your heart and intuition." Steve Jobs

"I want to standas close to the edge as I can without going over. Out on the edge you see all the kinds of things you can't see from the center." Kurt Vonnegut

"No one is dumb who is curious. Th people who don't ask questions remain clueless throughout their lives" Neil deGrasse Tyson

"Some people see things that are and ask, Why? Some people dream of things that never were and ask, Why not? Some people have to go to work and don't have time for all that." George Carlin

"Really, the only thing that makes sense is to strive for greater collective enlightenment." Elon Musk

"The problem is, God gave man a brain and a penis and only enough blood to run one at a time" Robin Williams

"I am tired and sick of war. Its glory is all moonshine. It is only those who have never fired a shot nor heard the shrieks and groans of the wounded who cry aloud for blood, for vengeance, for desolation. War is hell." William Tecumseh Sherman

"On the whole, human beings want to be good, but not too good, and not quite all the time." George Orwell

Warning: Material may cause you to think and read. Also, if you become offended or laugh out loud or say "I can't believe they actually wrote that" then you are actively engaged and learning, so enjoy becoming Absolutely Vocabulous ™

Absolutely Vocabulous — obfuscate

If it wasn't his only job offer, newly minted University of Virginia Law graduate Saul M.Y. Briefs would have quit when a senior partner informed him, even before he got in the front door, that "**obfuscation**" is a lawyer's best friend.

Yes, Sir, certainly my first set of shell corporations will have at least 3 in the Caymans. Happy Tax Vacation.

obfuscate: render obscure, unclear, or unintelligible; becloud
Synonym: Becloud   Say What? ob-fuhs-keyt   Antonym: Clarify

©2020 AbVocab Publishing, Inc. www.facebook.com/abvocab   www.abvocab.com   AbVocab™ with SketchiToons®

Resolute

Despite being ridiculed for having a nine-tailed demon fox spirit trapped in his body, Naruto Uzumaki was **resolute** to become the leader of Hokage. He goes on to own Kurama 100% and the Chakra of all the beasts tails!

Resolute: admirably purposeful & determined
   Synonym: Unyielding   Antonym: Timid
   Say What? reh-zuh-loot   BOM 2

I am Naruto, believe it!

Encroach-Photosynthesis

The race for the biggest canopy was on. It was win or go home. The 2 oak trees scratched and clawed trying to compete for sunlight. They each thought the other was encroaching on what was rightfully theirs. Their best strategy was photosynthesis but other strategies included heckling, trying to block sunlight, sending vines and weeds up the other tree, throwing sticks or mutating into a skeleton.

Encroach: intrude on a person's territory
    Synonym: Infringe   Antonym: Ignore
    Say What? ehn-krowch   BOM 2

Photosynthesis: trees and plants use energy from sunlight and C02 from the air to make the food they need to live and grow

Photsynthesis is not working, time to throw sticks!

Insatiable-Covet

Ponce De Leon & the insatiable conquistadors went for the world record of assholery by bringing slaves & smallpox to the new world and simultaneously coveting the Fountain of Youth so I guess they could keep on being cruel forever. The irony of searching for the fountain of youth in Florida, presently the senior citizen epicenter, is not lost on AdVocab.

Insatiable: a desire impossible to satisfy
    Synonym: Unsatisfied   Antonym: Fullfilled
    Say What? in-sei-shuh-bl   BOM 2

Covet: yearn to possess or have something
    Synonym: Desire   Antonym: Renounce
    Say what? kuhv-it   BOM 2

Irony: when actions have an effect exactly opposite from what is intended

I guess the Conquistadors were expecting this? Clearly not mental Giants

Conquistador: a Spanish conqueror
Fountain of Youth: a spring that restores youth if you bathe or drink its water. Sure it does.

11

Absolutely Vocabulous — olfactory BOM 3

Hired by perfume company Chanel for his extreme **olfactory** capabilities, Pinocchio was promptly fired when his long standing issues with veracity were raised by the press and sales dropped 50%. Who needs to a proverbial liar?

"I'm Brad Pitt. For Chanel. A quality product. Smells good too."

olfactory : relating to sense of smell   Inspired by BHH
Synonym: Aromatic   Say What? ol-fak-tuh-ree   Antonym: Odorless

©2020 AbVocab Publishing, Inc. www.facebook.com/abvocab   www.abvocab.com   AbVocab™ with SketchiToons®

Attenuate

To try to **attenuate** her husband's bad temper, Jane would randomly bring him a sandwich. This worked wonders. He's so simple she thought. "Oh come on, make the shot, you are right in front of the goal, I'm so angry… ooooh, is that balogna & cheese?"

Attenuate: to reduce force, effect, or value
  Synonym: Weaken   Antonym: Strengthen
  Say What? uh-ten-yoo-eyt   BOM 3

Boisterous-Jarring-Reverberate

The boisterous middle school band was a disaster. There was some jarring noise coming from the flute section. The clarinet section produced one collective squeal as if they forgot how to put a reed on properly. The kids in the trombone section sounded like they were competing for last chair. Finally, the base percussion section reverberated the whole auditorium.

Boisterous: noisy, energetic, and cheerful
    Synonym: Rowdy   Antonym: Quiet
    Say What? boi-ster-uhs   BOM 2
Jarring: incongruous in a striking way
    Synonym: Clashing   Antonym: Smooth
    Say What? jahr-ing   BOM 2
Reverberate: vibrate in sound
    Synonym: Echo   Antonym: Deaden
    Say What? ri-vur-buh-reyt   BOM 2

Boisterous & jarring squeal coming from the middle school band

I know they are just kids but my God, but do they actually practice these instruments during class?

Artisanal-Fastidious

If you haven't experienced an Amish broom, you are missing a core element in the cleaning experience. The broom-corn, AKA sorghum, is tightly woven and spun in a machine. It is worth paying up for this artisanal delight because I want to say with some confidence that you can get up oh I'd say 1/3 more dirt per sweep than the average broom, it's more durable & you will have the relief of knowing that a pair of fastidious & strong Amish hands made it.

Artisan: a worker in a skilled trade
    Synonym: Craftsperson   Antonym: Novice
    Say What? ahr-tuh-zuh n   BOM 3
Fastidious: attentive to accuracy & detail
    Synonym: Exacting   Antonym: Careless
    Say What? fa-sti-dee-uhs   BOM 3

Artisinal Delight that you won't find at Walmart.

One quick glance and you know that this artisanal broom was made from strong & fastidious Amish hands.

Absolutely Vocabulous overzealous

Sergeant Krupke and Lieutenant Schrank were **overzealous** in their attempt to arrest kids involved in graffiti and tagging activities in downtown Manhattan.

That perp in red! Over There! She's taking to the Lam!

We need Backup!

This one here. To the Big house!

overzealous: overly devoted to pursuit of a cause or objective
Synonym: Aggressive   Say What? oh-ver-zel-uhs   Antonym: Restrained

©2020 AbVocab Publishing, Inc. www.facebook.com/abvocab   www.abvocab.com   AbVocab™ with SketchiToons®

Aerobic

Lance Armstrong has incredible aerobic capacity. During the Tour de France, when others were gasping for air, he seemed to not even be winded. It sure helps having a heart 1/3 larger than average!

Aerobic: requiring oxygen
   Synonym: Endurance   Antonym: Anaerobic
   Say What? ai-roh-bik   BOM 3

Lance is tough as nails but it sure helps to have a massive heart!

Pugnacious-Immortalize-Lionize

The movie "Rocky 4" features a 5'9" Philly southpaw boxer whose first line of defense is his face matched up against a pugnacious 6'6" Russian Olympic champion Ivan Drago. After Rocky gets pummeled in the face repeatedly by Drago's superpunch, Rocky somehow manages to will his way to victory. Philadelphians were so excited by this that they immortalized their fictional champ with a statue. Even when pointing out to them that Rocky would have gotten his ass kicked in a real matchup with Drago, they nonetheless still lionize him to this day.

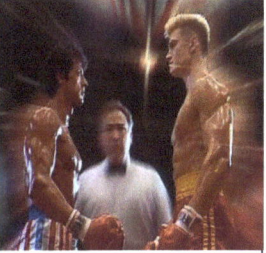

Does this look like a fair match up to you?

Rocky getting pummeled in the face by Drago's superpunch

Pugnacious: eager or quick to argue or fight
    Synonym: Aggressive   Antonym: Tame
    Say What? puhg-nei-shuhs   BOM 3

Immortalized: confer enduring fame upon
    Synonym: Commemorate   Antonym: Ignore
    Say What? i-mor-tuh-laizd   BOM 2

Lionize: celebrate
    Synonym: Glorify   Antonym: Condemn
    Say What? lai-uh-naiz   BOM 3

Smoldering-Alleviate

After the previous night at the bar, Butch the bodybuilding brute bouncer wanted a pay raise. In 4 hours he had to disarm a man with a bow and arrow, extinguish a smoldering fire in the pool room, alleviate a fight between a cat woman chick vs. a ninja warrior & had to referee the arm wrestling contest as well as a sumo wrestling contest.

"I need a pay raise after last night. I had to run in and break up this fight."

Smolder: to burn slowly with smoke
    Synonym: Simmer   Antonym: Freeze
    Say What? smohl-der   BOM 2

Alleviate: make a problem less severe
    Synonym: Ease   Antonym: Worsen
    Say What? uh-lee-vee-yet   BOM 2

Absolutely Vocabulous — plethora  BOM 2

Jed inherited a 500 acre area with a protected mountain spring. I'm a rich dude now! This expectation was squashed when he saw the **plethora** of bottled water brands even at the convenience store. His daughter reminded him that the brand Evian was naive spelled backwards. Smart ass indeed.

plethora: a large or excessive amount of something
Synonym: Glut   Say What? pleth-er-uh   Antonym: Scarcity

©2020 AbVocab Publishing, Inc. www.facebook.com/abvocab   www.abvocab.com   AbVocab™ with SketchiToons®

Unscathed

Hormingo, the pavement ant, told the ultimate war story to his buddies once back safely under the concrete. Well, first I got my thorax stuck on the hot pavement and couldn't move. Then it started raining and I almost drowned. Finally, the little boy who lives in the house started crushing ants by stomping on them and chipped my mandible. Somehow I got out unscathed!

Unscathed: without suffering any harm
   Synonym: Unharmed   Antonym: Harmed
   Say What? uhn-skeithd   BOM 2

"I can't believe I came out unscathed."

Menagerie

Walmart is quite the menagerie. At this one stop shop you can witness aisles of pre-packaged goods, scantily clad women, throngs of obese shoppers trying to locate that high carb low price deal, screaming toddlers in their terrible 2's, senior citizens lost in the produce isle, flash mobs looting, petty domestic disputes, vampires, drunk sailors and much much more.

Menagerie: a strange or diverse collection of people or things
    Synonym: Zoo   Antonym: Organized
    Say What? muh-naj-uh-ree   BOM 3
Throng- a large, densely packed crowd of people

Old lady who thinks she's in auto parts. Is that a vampire?

Industrious-Bustling-Intricate

Uttar was an industrious hustler from Bangladesh. He was a modest man trying to make ends meet. He woke up at 4 AM every morning and loaded up his wares on his traveling cart and took to the bustling streets. Uttar could get you anything you wanted. His cart was lined intricately with tomatoes, cigarettes, magazines, bread, beef and much more. If you sent him a request he could magically get that item the next day. At night he drove people around on his rickshaw. Uttar's the man.

Industrious: diligent and hard working
    Synonym: Diligent   Antonym: Lazy
    Say What? in-duh-stree-uhs   BOM 2
Bustling: full of activity
    Synonym: Teeming   Antonym: Empty
    Say What? buhs-uhl   BOM 2
Intricate: very complicated or detailed
    Synonym: Convoluted   Antonym: Simple
    Say What? in-trah-kuht   BOM 2

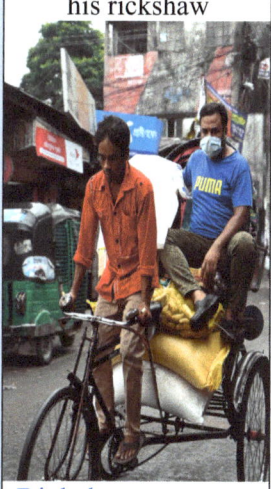

Industrious Uttar driving someone on his rickshaw

Rickshaw- a light two-wheeled vehicle drawn by one or more people, used chiefly in Asian countries

Absolutely Vocabulous — precarious

BOM 2

Once Janice realized she was to meet Her Royal Majesty, aka the Queen, and may have to bow or curtsey with some decorum, she realized that her dress choice put her in a precarious situation that might lead to her mortification.

precarious: not securely held in position; likely to fall or collapse; lack of stability
Synonym: Hazardous   Say What? pri-kair-ee-uhs   Antonym: Secure

©2020 AbVocab Publishing, Inc. www.facebook.com/abvocab   www.abvocab.com   AbVocab™ with SketchiToons®

Reveling-Reverie

Oh, the thought of reveling on a warm beach in the summer, listening to Jimmy Buffett while drinking a margarita and havana daydreaming, as the kids make sand castles makes me smile. Then reality sets in, ruining my reverie.

Revel: take pleasure in
   Synonym: Bask   Antonym: Gloom
   Say What? rev-uhl   BOM 2

Reverie: pleasantly lost in one's thoughts
   Synonym: Daydream   Antonym: Nightmare
   Say What? rev-uh-ree   BOM 2

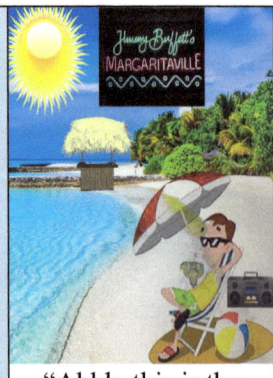

"Ahhh, this is the life."

Encapsulates

Nothing encapsulates the era of pseudoscience, misinformation & celebrity culture better than Kyrie Irving proclaiming that the earth is flat. Neil Degrasse Tyson calmly gave about 10 reasons why he was wrong, 1 for example that in a solar eclipse you can see the earth's shadow on the moon and it is round but sadly many kids will who idolize Kyrie will believe him over Tyson.

Encapsulate: express the essential features of something succinctly
    Synonym: Summarize   Antonym: Expand
    Say What? en-kap-suh-leyt   BOM 3

Tyson losing his patience with Kyrie spewing flat earth pseudoscience

Pseudoscience- beliefs mistakenly regarded as being real science

Tantalizing-Freewheeling-Tenacious

At the circus you will find agile acrobats, creepy clowns, vigorous ventriloquists, mesmerizing magicians, jazzy jugglers, tantalizing tightrope walkers, freewheeling fire eaters, tenacious trapeze artists, graceful gymnasts & marvelous mime artists. Quite the motley crew I would say.

Tantalize: torment or tease someone with something that is unobtainable
    Synonym: Instigate   Antonym: Repel
    Say What? tan-tl-ahyz   BOM 2

Freewheeling: characterized by a disregard for rules or conventions
    Synonym: Liberated   Antonym: Fettered
    Say What? free-hwee-ling   BOM 2

Tenacious: not readily relinquishing a position, principle, or course of action
    Synonym: Persistent   Antonym: Yield
    Say What? tuh-ney-shuhs

Motley Crew Indeed!

You should always be prepared to be slightly weirded out at the "Greatest Show on Earth"

Absolutely Vocabulous — inimical — BOM 3

The ACLU has filed a class action suit for Bulls and Chickens charging that the terms 'Bull Shit' and 'Chicken Shit' are belittling, demeaning and most importantly lead to actions **inimical** to their clients. Stay Woke.

My shit may be small, but I protect my eggs with ferocious claws!

I may pass a lot of it, but it's honestly done. Never a doubt when I'm Pissed!

inimical: tending to obstruct or harm
Synonym: Adverse   **Say What?** ih-nim-i-kuhl   **Antonym:** Favorable

©2020 AbVocab Publishing, Inc. www.facebook.com/abvocab   www.abvocab.com   AbVocab™ with SketchiToons®

Opiates-Nadir

George became addicted to **opiates** after undergoing surgery. When his prescription ran out he started using heroin. His family left him and he started visiting the red light district in town. This was the **nadir** of his life.

Opiate: medicine used for pain relief
    Synonym: Narcotic   Antonym: Stimulant
    Say What? oh-pee-it   BOM 2

Nadir: the lowest point in fortunes
    Synonym: Rock Bottom   Antonym: Top
    Say What? ney-deer   BOM 2

Red Light District where George frequented after he got on the smack

20

Illicit

Let's talk for a sec about weed. In the 1800's weed became accepted in mainstream medicine & use. During the Great Depression, people were worried about Mexican immigrants taking their jobs. So, the US Gov't started a disinformation campaign to associate Mexicans with weed in the minds of the US people. Once people were scared, the **propaganda** pill was easily swallowed & weed became **illicit**.

Illicit: something against the law
- Synonym: Illegal   Antonym: Allowed
- Say What? ih-lis-it   BOM 2

Illicit because it's dangerous or because of who is using it?

Propaganda: information that is designed to mislead or persuade

Infiltrate-Incursion-Engorge

In Attila the Hun fashion, 30 Japanese hornets **infiltrated** a nest of 30,000 European honeybees and were able to massacre the entire colony. This **incursion** only took 5 minutes! Add insult to injury, they **engorged** themselves on the honey and then took the larvae & pupae home to feed their young.

Infiltrate- enter a place to secretly to acquire information
- Synonym: Penetrate   Antonym: Escape
- Say What? in-fil-treyt   BOM 2

Incursion- sudden or brief invasion
- Synonym: Raid   Antonym: Retreat
- Say What? in·kur·zhn   BOM 2

Engorge- eat to excess
- Synonym: Stuff   Antonnym: Nibble
- Say What? ehn·gorj   BOM 2

Not cool hornets. Pick on something your own size!

Attila the Hun- ruler of the Huns from 434 until his death in March 453, rumored to have killed millions of people.

21

Absolutely Vocabulous   quandary   BOM 3

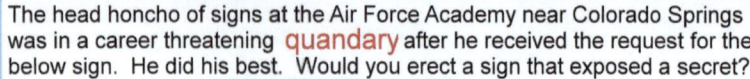

The head honcho of signs at the Air Force Academy near Colorado Springs was in a career threatening quandary after he received the request for the below sign. He did his best. Would you erect a sign that exposed a secret?

quandary: state of uncertainty over what to do next in a difficult situation
Synonym: Dilemma   Say What? kwon-duh-ree   Antonym: Solution

©2020 AbVocab Publishing, Inc. www.facebook.com/abvocab   www.abvocab.com   AbVocab™ with SketchiToons®

Pertinacious

Fossil evidence shows that cockroaches have been around for 300 millions years. So why are these pertinacious insects tough to kill? Well, they can live without their heads for weeks, they are great at changing gears when running almost as if they have stick shift transmission, they can make group decisions, live without food for a month, live in walls, & can bite!

Pertinacious - holding firmly to a course of action
    Synonym: Resolute   Antonym: Wavering
    Say What? pur-tn-ey-shuhs   BOM 4

Perinacious little suckers ain't they.

Fossil Evidence: dating used to determine a fossils age

Occlude

So, you are talking with friends while you drink your sprite and your friend tells a hilarious penis joke. You start laughing and then you start choking. What exactly happened there? Well, the sprite is supposed to go down your esophagus (throat). There is a little flap called the epiglottis that occludes your trachea (windpipe) to ensure that the sprite goes down your throat but not your trachea. But, if you are laughing, your epiglottis screws up and the sprite gets in the trachea, which is where air is supposed to go. This causes a cough reflex. So, lets give some props to the epiglottis next time you can eat and breathe at the same time.

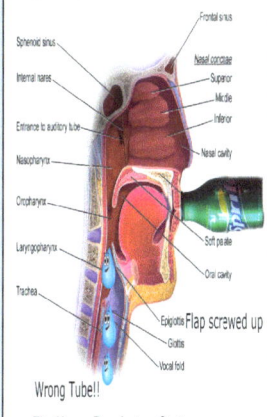

Wrong Tube!!
The Upper Respiratory System

Occlude - obstruct an opening or passage
    Synonym: Block   Antonym: Open
    Say What? uh-klood   BOM 2

So, sprite and laughing from penis joke= epiglottis getting jarred= sprite down trachea=choke

Fiasco

Nathan was dancing with his heartthrob Rebecca at Prom. He was completely sprung. Unfortunately, another thing was being sprung. After a slow dance, his date decided she needed to get a drink from the punch bowl leading him by the hand across the entire dance floor and everyone couldn't help but notice the bulge below his pants. He quickly tried to pull the under the belt maneuver but it was too late. This was a fiasco.

Fiasco - a thing that is a complete failure, especially in a ludicrous or humiliating way
    Synonym: Blunder   Antonym: Miracle
    Say What? fee-as-koh   BOM 2

Oh god, not a slow dance, this can't be happening. Absolute fiasco.

Absolutely Vocabulous: quid pro quo

Crocodiles let plover birds pick leeches off their gums. A basic biological, as opposed to political, quid pro quo. In this mutualistic symbiotic relationship, the croc opens its mouth - wide - and the bird lunches on the parasitic leeches.

"Nolita here never opens without a fuss."

"Lovely Leech Lunch!"

quid pro quo: a favor or advantage granted with something expected in return
Synonym: Tit For Tat   Say What? kwid-proh-kwoh   Antonym: Pro Bono
©2020 AbVocab Publishing, Inc. www.facebook.com/abvocab   www.abvocab.com   AbVocab™ with SketchiToons®

Debacle

The first colonists arrived at Jamestown in 1607 as the first permanent English colony. They quickly realized things were going to get rough. Surrounded by Powhatans & starving to death, they resorted to cannibalism. That only bought some time. This was a complete debacle. Finally with their backs against the wall & shot clock running out in the 4th Quarter, a miracle. What was that miracle? Tobacco.

Debacle: a huge failure
    Synonym: Cataclysm   Antonym: Success
    Say What? dey-bah-kuhl   BOM 2

Tobacco Field

Miracle at Jamestown. This savior staved off starvation and collapse.

Contaminated-Sordid

After itching his scrotum in the hotel room, Ted sat on the end of the bed and grabbed the remote to check the weather for tomorrow. It never crossed his mind that every single person had done the same thing before him. We all know the lower sheets get washed but sadly, the top sheet, quilt & remote more than likely stay contaminated for the next sordid guest.

Contaminate- make something impure by exposure to a poisonous or polluting substance
    Synonym: Taint   Antonym: Purify
    Say What? kuhn-tam-uh-neyt   BOM 2

Sordid- dirty or squalid
    Synonym: Dirty   Antonym: Clean
    Say What? sawr-did   BOM 2

Sadly, the top sheet and quilt more than likely stay contaminated

Doctrinaire-Pedantic

The doctrinaire math professor was starting to let his day job affect his personal life. His wife started to worry about him after she put dinner on the table and he pedantically asked her to show her work and he was concerned that she didn't do it in the right order.

Doctrinaire: impose doctrine but not practical
    Synonym: Dictatorial   Antonym: Flexible
    Say What? dok-truh-nair   BOM 3

Pedantic: concerned with minor details
    Synonym: Formal   Antonym: Informal
    Say What? peh-dnt   BOM 3

"Honey, the salad comes first in the equation, not the turkey so sadly you won't get full credit."

Prolific

Arnold Schwarzenegger's prolific feats include bodybuilding awards, movie star & Governor of California, enough success for 10 lifetimes.

Prolific: present in large numbers or quantities
    Synonym: Fruitful Antonym: Unproductive
    Say What? pruh-lif-ik   BOM 2

Absolutely Vocabulous   **quixotic**   BOM 3

Given their self-declared expert knowledge of vocabulary and related subjects, it is surprising that Matt Quenville and Sketchi Bill hired a salesman who described himself as quixotic and had as his last job title: 'chief tilter.'

Forget the effin' Windmills! Sell our damn Vocabulary Books!

SIR VENTES CASTLE KEEP EST. 1567

quixotic: foolishly romantic; unrealistic and impractical
Synonym: Fanciful   Say What? kwik-sot-ik   Antonym: Pragmatic
©2020 AbVocab Publishing, Inc. www.facebook.com/abvocab   www.abvocab.com   AbVocab™ with SketchiToons®

Squalid

Who would have thought that if you take wild exotic animals and let them sit in a squalid non-health inspected wet market for days in a densely populated city it may cause a virus to emerge?

Squalid: a place extremely dirty and unpleasant, especially as a result of neglect
    Synonym: Filthy   Antonym: Clean
    Say What? skwaa-luhd   BOM 2

Wet Market: a market selling fresh meat, fish, produce, and other perishable goods

Wait, so it's not a good idea to put a bunch of exotic animals in a squalid wet market?

Illustrious

Babe Ruth was sports first superstar. He became its most illustrious power hitter. However, here at Advocab we try to provoke. I dare say Babe Ruth would not even make a baseball team today. He played at a time when you had to be white, American, and not be fighting in the war. Also there were no curveballs or sliders & top pitch speed was 70 mph. And he was a drunk. And he was overweight. Yes, I know, you can't compare eras. But let's just take down the hype a bit on the sultan of swat.

Illustrious: well known, respected, and admired for past achievements

    Synonym: Distinguished Antonym: Ordinary
    Say What? ih-luhs-tree-uhs   BOM 3

The Great Bambino hanging out with a couple of flappers at a speakeasy before a big game.

Frigid-Pristine

Southerners don't quite realize just how friggin frigid the tundra is. Sure it may look pristine with the white snow and all from the outside but it is absolute misery to live in. Do you have to start your car 30 minutes before leaving to go anywhere? You Betcha. Do you have to take 20 minutes to get warm clothes on your kids before leaving the house? Oh yah. Do you have to shovel snow out of your driveway every day. Oh sure. That shits tough, ya know.

Frigid: very cold in temperature
    Synonym: Cold   Antonym: Hot
    Say What? Frijid   BOM 2
Pristine: in its original condition
    Synonym: Clean   Antonym: Dirty
    Say What? pruh-steen   BOM 2

"One Second kids, just have to shovel this car out."

Tundra- a vast, flat, treeless Arctic region in which the subsoil is permanently frozen

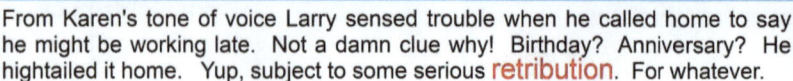

retribution

From Karen's tone of voice Larry sensed trouble when he called home to say he might be working late. Not a damn clue why! Birthday? Anniversary? He hightailed it home. Yup, subject to some serious retribution. For whatever.

"Honey. Your animosity directed at that carrot. Urrh. I guess I'll be sleeping on the sofa for awhile!"

Ziiiip.

retribution: punishment as vengeance for a wrong or criminal act
Synonym: Payback   Say What? re-truh-byoo-shuhn   Antonym: Forgiveness

©2020 AbVocab Publishing, Inc. www.facebook.com/abvocab www.abvocab.com AbVocab™ with SketchiToons®

Notorious

Bullet ants are notorious gangsters. The pain of getting stung by one is described as blinding, electric pain, comparable to being shot with a gun or walking over a flaming charcoal with a 3-inch nail embedded in your heel. Native to South America, the Sateré-Mawé people of Brazil use bullet ant stings as part of their initiation rites to become warriors. Whoa!

The Mawe stick their hands into gloves that contain 100's of bullet ants.

Notorious: famous for bad reasons
   Synonym: Infamous   Antonym: Famous
   Say What? noh-tawr-ee-uhs   BOM 2

Abscond

Greg has just finished putting his perfectly grilled Porterhouse steak on the kitchen table and turned his back for 10 seconds. Cleo the Black Lab ran up and grabbed the steak from the counter. Greg tried to catch him but Cleo absconded out the doggie door away from danger.

Abscond: leave hurriedly to avoid detection
    Synonym: Flee   Antonym: Arrive
    Say What? ab-skond   BOM 2

Cleo being an asshole. Before I could grab the steak he absconded out the doggie door!

Contentious-Balkanize

The contentious futbol hooligans in Europe were balkanized based on which team they supported. With breathtaking stupidity, these barbarians want to attack fans of other teams in an ultimate act of tribalism.

Contentious: causing an argument
    Synonym: Quarrelsome   Antonym: Calm
    Say what? kuhn-ten-shuhs   BOM 2
Balkanize: divide into smaller hostile groups
    Synonym: Grouped   Antonym: Mixed
    Say What? baal-kuh-naiz   BOM 2

Hooligans fighting over a sport smh.

Tribalism: behavior and attitudes that stem from strong loyalty to one's own tribe or social group

Capitulate

Supergirl is like a hybrid between Superman and the Flash. She also possesses super senses, super freeze breath, as well as various forms of vision. You won't find her capitulating to Silver Banchee.

Capitulate- cease to resist an opponent or an unwelcome demand
    Synonym: Surrender   Antonym: Fight
    Say What? kuh-pich-uh-leyt   BOM 2

Supergirl never capitulates.

 **belligerent**

Angela realized too late that John Michael's watching of TCN (Trump Cartoon Network) gave him the idea that a *belligerent* approach was best. Attack. Lie. Intimidate. Revile. Repeat...Repeat...until GROUNDED!

John. Mrs. White said you hit the ball through her window. Did you?

The video she sent shows you aiming to hit the window.

Fred is away on vacation.

You are Grounded!

That's a nasty question!

Fred did it.

I have a BAT!!

YOU ARE A TERRIBLE MOTHER!

belligerent: hostile and aggressive
Synonym: pugnacious   Say What? buh-llj-uhr-ruhn   Antonym: peaceable
©2020 AbVocab Publishing, Inc. www.facebook.com/abvocab   www.abvocab.com   AbVocab™ with SketchiToons®

Unorthodox

Sick of being called obese, Roland tried a very unorthodox but painful way to lose weight. By placing his desires just out of reach, he thought he could overcome them.

Unorthodox: contrary to what is usual, traditional, or accepted
    Synonym: Abnormal   Antonym: Usual
    Say What? uhn-awr-thuh-doks   BOM 2

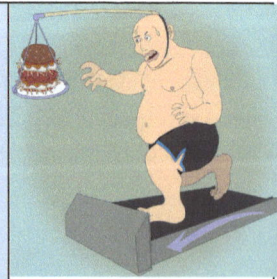

"I'm not hungry!"

Exculpate

Ignaz Semmelwies said that doctors should wash their hands before delivering babies. For this, he was taken to an insane asylum and beat to death. It was thought that "gentlemen" don't have dirty hands. He was fully exculpated later on when Joseph Lister proved that the infant mortality rate would plummet if hands were washed and surgery equipment sterilized.

Exculpate: to show or declare that someone is not guilty of wrongdoing
    Synonym: Absolve   Antonym: Blame
    Say What? ek-skuhl-peyt   BOM 3

Infant Mortality- the death of children under the age of 1 year

Hey, is it too much to ask that you wash your hands before delivering babies?

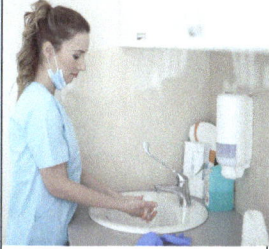

Amazing that doctors didn't wash their hands until 1847.

Malevolent-Mythical-Bask

Jaws is a movie about a malevolent and mythical killer shark that prowls the beaches in a fictional island. This movie is one reason people are terrified of sharks. But, people are really bad at statistics. You have a 1 and 265 million chance of being killed by a shark. Just sticking to the beach theme, driving to the beach, laying out basking in the sun's rays, drowning & getting caught in a sand hole collapse are all much more dangerous than a shark. Shark phobia is nonsense!

Malevolent: having a wish to do evil to others
    Synonym: Sinister   Antonym: Benign
    Say What? muh-leh-vuh-luhnt   BOM 3

Mythical: characteristic of myths or folk tales
    Synonym: Make-Believe   Antonym: Real
    Say What? mith-i-kuh l   BOM 2

Bask: lie exposed to warmth from the sun
    Synonym: Sunbathe   Antonym: Cover
    Say What? Bahsk   BOM 1

Baby Jaws eating a boat, no biggie

This is not looking good for this girl

Absolutely Vocabulous — ecstacy

Britney and Katy sang 'Roar' and 'Baby One More Time' as they knocked over a few trashcans and terrorized the folks at a food truck. They were **ecstatic** because they got to eat their favorite flavors of ice cream.

BIRTHDAY TWINS

"Don't need to wear those lame party hats anymore"

"They sure did run when we started dragging out those bbq rib bones."

ecstasy: an overwhelming feeling of great happiness or excitement
Synonym: Enraptured   Say What? ek-stat-ik   Antonym: Depressed

©2020 AbVocab Publishing, Inc. www.facebook.com/abvocab   www.abvocab.com   AbVocab™ with SketchiToons®

Totalitarian-Admonition

Jessica installed a **totalitarian** dictatorship in her playroom. Under no circumstance could any other children play with her barbies, dollhouse or toys. If they tried, they were greeted with a stiff arm to the head & a harsh **admonition**.

Totalitarian: relating to a system of government that is centralized and dictatorial
  Synonym: Tyrannical   Antonym: Democratic
  Say What? toh-tal-i-tair-ee-uh n   BOM 2

Admonition: to give a warning
  Synonym: Caution   Antonym: Allow
  Say What? ad-muh-nish-uh n   BOM 2

"It's mine, all of it"

Jessica ruling the play room with an iron fist.

Staunch-Conscience

The libertarian lifeguard sat and watched the people drown in the pool. Part of him wanted to jump in and save lives, but because he was such a staunch believer in freedom, his conscience would not let him interfere. "Well, they chose to jump in knowing they couldn't swim so that's on them".

Staunch: loyal and committed in attitude
    Synonym: Loyal   Antonym: Waffle
    Say What? stawnch   BOM 2

Conscience: an inner feeling or voice acting as a moral guide of one's behavior
    Synonym: Moral Compass
    Say What? kaan-shns   BOM 2

These people were free to swim and I'm free to sit here and let them drown.

Libertarian- one who seeks to maximize political freedom.

Impropriety-Prurient

Jaden was a hormone raging 8th grader. He was not atypical in his interest in all things sexual. He tried to control this impropriety but it was difficult when it was everywhere he looked. The kids talked about it at school & it was all over the Internet and in his mind. His parents knew that the only way to distract his prurient interests was to flood him with activities like sports, clubs & school work. But even in chess class he was day dreaming of it.

Impropriety: improper language, behavior, or character
    Synonym: Indecency   Antonym: Decent
    Say What? im-pruh-prai-uh-tee   BOM 3

Prurient: excessive interest in sexual matters
    Synonym: lewd   Antonym: Chaste
    Say What? proo-r-ee-uh-nt   BOM 3

"What is wrong with me? I even see a girl in a bikini when playing chess. When will this phase end?"

Hubris

If the 5 Billion year history of the earth were condensed into 1 calendar year, humans would have arrived on the scene in the last second. It would appear that an ass ton of anthropocentric hubris would be needed to think the earth was designed for humans. As you can see looking at the calendar, humans just arrived. Why are we so important again?

Hubris: excessive self-pride
   Synonym: Vain   Antonym: Humility
   Say What? hyoo-bris   BOM 3

Anthropocentric: regarding humankind as the most important

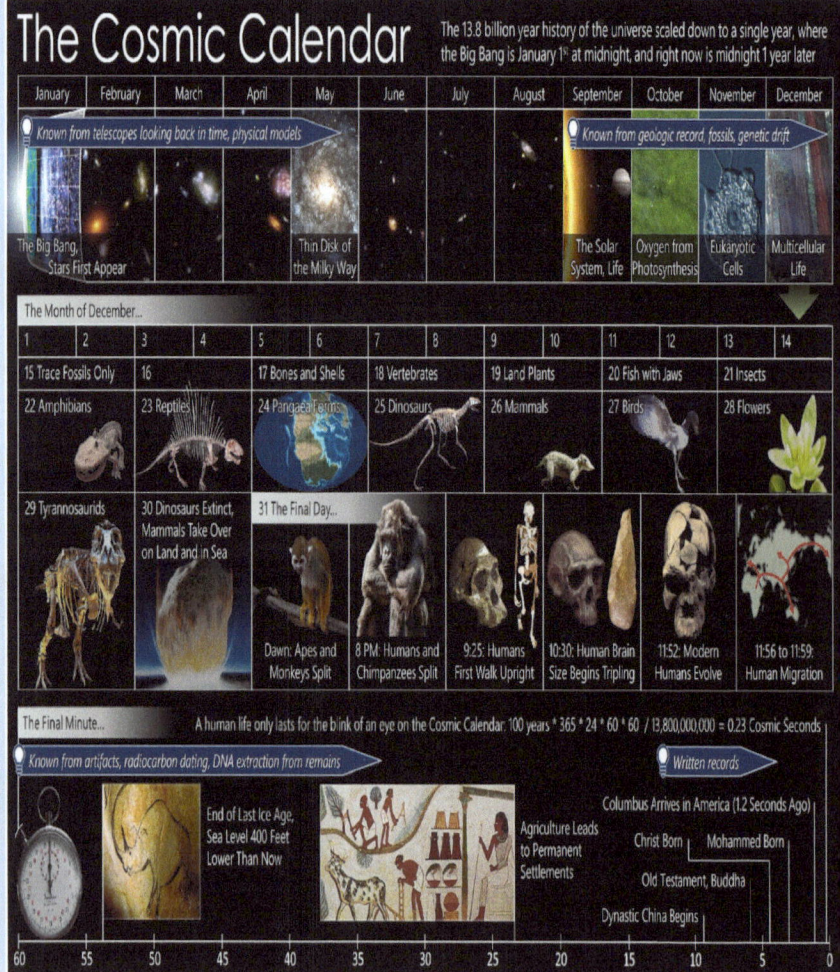

Tremulous

Alan gets 4 hours a sleep a night due to stress at work & sleep apnea. In the morning, he drinks 4 cups of coffee & pops a caffeine pill mixed with Adderall. He has a slightly tremulous demeanor & tends to stutter. This morning he saw an orca whale jump out of his coffee that appeared to have arms and legs. Am I going crazy he wondered?

Tremulous: shaking or quivering slightly
    Synonym: Quivering   Antonym: Calm
    Say What? reh-myuh-luhs   BOM 3

"wtf is going on? I need more sleep."

Belligerent

Martin the Marmoset kept fresh insects and lizards in the refrigerator. When he found out that his roomate ate the last gecko he became belligerent and kicked over the fridge.

Belligerent: hostile & aggressive
    Synonym: Hostile   Antonym: Docile
    Say What? buh-lij-er-uhnt   BOM 2

"Who eats the last Gecko!"

Assuage

Matthew woke up with a crippling hangover. He tried to wake up when his alarm went off but felt nothing but pain. That shit wasn't worth it he thought. He had heard about the hair of the dog so he said what the hell and rolled over to finish off the dregs of the beer from the night before to assuage the pain. Ahhh, feeling better already.

Assuage: to make an unpleasant feeling less intense
    Synonym: Allay   Antonym: Exacerbate
    Say What? uh-sweyj   BOM 2

"What was I thinking, I need a hair of the dog."

Hair Of The Dog: decrease effects of a hangover by drinking more alcohol.

Absolutely Vocabulous — exultation

Chihuahua Fang's feeling of **exultation** at kicking ass in a 'bark off' against Ira the rottweiler, kept him from registering that footsteps and other noises meant that the screen door would soon be open.

exultation: a feeling of triumphant joy or jubilation or delight
Synonym: Elation   Say What? ek-suhl-tAY-shuhn
©2020 AbVocab Publishing, Inc. www.facebook.com/abvocab   www.abvocab.com   AbVocab™ with SketchiToons®

Cherubic

Why are babies so cute? Maybe their cherubic appearance can help parents overlook their needy, selfish, crying, spitting, crapping selves.

Cherubic: having the childlike innocence or plump prettiness of a cherub
    Synonym: Angelic   Antonym: Demonic
    Say What? chuh-roo-bik   BOM 2

"I'm so cute! Now, change my diaper."

Chimera

The chimera in Sally's nightmare was so vivid. It was a dragon with wings and scaly, creepy skin. The more she tried to not think of it the more she dreamed of it. Finally, once she had the courage to kill the dragon, she stopped dreaming of it.

Chimera: a horrible or unreal creature of the imagination
    Synonym: Fantasy   Antonym: Reality
    Say What? ki-meer-uh   BOM 2

Sally finally defeated the chimera in her nightmare.

Auspicious

If we ever try to clone the perfect super-athlete, I would recommend a hybrid cross between Serena Williams & Lebron James. The product of that genetic engineering could just choose whatever sport they want to dominate. Can you think of a more auspicious set of genes than that?

Auspicious: conducive to success; favorable
    Synonym: Promising   Antonym: Ominous
    Say What? aw-spish-uh s   BOM 3
Gene: a unit of heredity which is transferred from a parent to offspring and is held to determine some characteristic of the offspring

Meet Serbron Willames. The first athlete to play 5 professional sports.

Disillusioned

The dog Ralph was determined to catch a mole under the ground so spent all day digging. He became disillusioned to come up empty.

Disillusioned: disappointed in someone or something that one discovers to be less good than one had believed
    Synonym: Bitter   Antonym: Encouraged
    Say What? di-suh-loo-zhnd   BOM 2

Oh come on, why can't I catch this stinkin' mole.

Absolutely Vocabulous — inundated

The coronavirus spread quickly through the United States with the result that hospitals, morgues, and cemeteries were **inundated** before 'shutdowns' were effected. With early re-openings, lax personal adherence to guidelines, the first wave has regained traction late June. Stay tuned for results.

inundated: overwhelm with people, things or problems to be dealt with
Synonym: Swamp   Say What? In-uhn-dayt   Antonym: Drain

©2020 AbVocab Publishing, Inc. www.facebook.com/abvocab www.abvocab.com AbVocab™ with SketchiToons®

Skeptical

Larry told me he won the marathon. I was very skeptical until I found out that there were no Kenyans in the race and only 20 people competed.

Skeptical: not easily convinced; having doubts
   Synonym: Dubious   Antonym: Believing
   Say What? skep-ti-kuhl   BOM 2

Tough competition huh?

Enthrall-Rarified-Renowned

Brazilian soccer phenom Neymar has enthralled fans from around the world. His rarified skillset includes great acceleration, speed, dribbling, finishing and ability with both feet, which is probably why he signed with Real Madrid when he was only 14 years old. He is a renowned in the favelas in Brazil and has drawn comparisons to the great Pele.

Enthrall: to capture the fascinated attention of
　　Synonym: Enchant　　Antonym: Repel
　　Say What? ehn-thraal　　　　　　BOM 2

Rarified: exlusive, rare & special ability
　　Synonym: Special　　Antonym: Usual
　　Say What? rair-uh-fahyd　　　　BOM 2

Renowned: known by many people
　　Synonym: Famous　　Antonym: Ordinary
　　Say What? ri-nound　　　　　　BOM 2

Sorry Haters, I just can't stop scoring.

Legend in the Favellas

Favela- a shantytown located within Brazil

Probity

Who doesn't love Quakers? They have consistently shown probity on all issues, believed in equality long before others, thought slavery was a moral evil, thought women should have equal rights and William Penn has a cool looking wig.

Probity: having strong moral principles
　　Synonym: Integrity　　Antonym: Dishonest
　　Say What? prow-buh-tee　　　　BOM 2

Quaker: a member of the Religious Society of Friends, a Christian movement devoted to peaceful principles

Founder of Pennsylvania William Penn rocking wicked cool wig

Absolutely Vocabulous **literally** BOM 1

Are humans really more evolved than Pavlov's dog? Taking a constitutional without using the bathroom first, John had to rush home. His body conditioned that the relief was just inside the door. Key in lock. Doesn't turn. OMG. Well, Shit, **literally**. John lives in 5D next door.

literal: taking words precisely as they are; no metaphor or allegory
Synonym: Actually   Say What? lit-er-uh-lee   Antonym: Figuratively
©2020 AbVocab Publishing, Inc. www.facebook.com/abvocab   www.abvocab.com   AbVocab™ with SketchiToons®

Novice

When you are a novice, aka noob and begin playing Minecraft, you will get defeated. Noobs try to hug creepers, get cursed by witches, battle-axed by vindicators, squished by slime & arrowed by skeletons. Just look at this noob: He has no idea what to do in the Nether Portal. Notch would be disappointed. But Noobs wouldn't know who Notch is.

Novice: a person new to or inexperienced in a field or situation

    Synonym: Neophyte   Antonym: Expert
    Say What? nov-is   BOM 2

You think a novice will know what to do in the Nether Portal? They would probably try to break obsidian with wooden pick axe rotfl.

Ostensible

Condoms are ostensibly 99% effective so any oops babies probably means you can't follow the directions very well or you are in the unlucky 1%.

Ostensible: appearing to be true
    Synonym: Purported   Antonym: Unlikely
    Say What? o-sten-suh-buh l   BOM 3

If u still have an oops baby, you are unlucky indeed

Impetuous

The impetuous teenager decided to test the limits of his new whip and race another testosterone fueled rebel in a street race.

Impetuous: acting quickly without thought
    Synonym: Impulsive   Antonym: Thoughtful
    Say What? uhm-peh-choo-uhs   BOM 3

Impetuous teen racing. YOLO!

Simile

A bikini is like a barbed wire fence. It protects the property without obstructing the view.

Simile: comparison using like or as
    Synonym: Analogy   Antonym: Incongruous
    Say What? sim-uh-lee   BOM 2

Ambivalent

People tend to be ambivalent about the effect of technology on people. On the one hand, they have unlimited access to information in a split second but if used unproductively, it may just turn them into a generation of anti-social cyber-surfers that think virtual reality is real life.

Ambivalent: mixed feelings about something
    Synonym: Equivocal   Antonym: Certain
    Say What? am-bi-vuh-luhnt   BOM 3

Oh man, never going back to regular life.

Absolutely Vocabulous lurid

Rebecca told friend Stacy the **lurid** ambiance of the basement frat party. Kids just hooking up on the stairs. Everclear mixed with something like prune juice. And, OMG, the putrid smell from the beer flooded floor. Jim's feet dripping wet.

You guys use this room as a morgue recently?

Did they mix the beer with sweat and ass cheese?

Eww, your foot is going to be in that stuff soon.

lurid: vividly shocking especially explicit details of crime or sex
Synonym: Grisly   Say What? loor-id   Antonym: Clean
©2020 AbVocab Publishing, Inc. www.facebook.com/abvocab www.abvocab.com AbVocab™ with SketchiToons®

Platitude

"Grab a bull by the horns" is a commonly heard **platitude** about confronting tough problems in life. But can we at least make the analogy realistic. First of all, do you know how hard it would be to actually grab a bull by its horns? Do you think it would just willingly submit to this act? Next time you see a 2500 pound angry bull, try to go grab its horns and see if you remain in 1 piece after it's over.

Platitude: an unoriginal & overused saying
   Synonym: Cliché   Antonym: Original
   Say What? plat-i-tood   BOM 2

Grab Life By the Horns

Nonchalant

I don't know about you, but I like planet Earth. Instead of talking about colonizing Mars, why don't we stop screwing with this planet? Whoever is nonchalantly throwing any ole shit whereever they please, can u knock it off?
Nonchalant: appearing casually relaxed
    Synonym: Indifferent   Antonym: Concerned
    Say What? non-shuh-lahnt   BOM 2

Don't pollute nonchalantly or chalantly ok.

Indefatigable

The female weaver spider was having a tough day. She had worked indefatigably to make a giant orb web at her house in the tree. It was big enough to catch a few crickets for dinner & lay some eggs. Just when she finally finished, a huge gust of wind blew it down. She was indignant "I have to start over again!"
Indefatigable: a person persisting tirelessly
    Synonym: Untiring   Antonym: Tiring
    Say What? in-de-fa-tuh-guh-bl   BOM 3

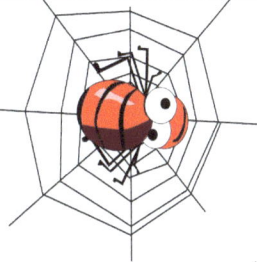

Okay, I weaved this web again after the last one got destroyed.

Braggadocio-Humility

Usain Bolt is fast as hell. In fact, he is the fastest runner to ever live. This Jamaican may come across as a bit of a braggadocio, but when you can run 27 miles per hour, which is faster than the speed limit in residential zones, humility becomes optional.
Braggadocio: boastful or arrogant
    Synonym: Blowhard   Antonym: Meek
    Say What? brag-uh-doh-shee-oh   BOM 2
Humility: a low view of one's own importance
    Synonym: Humble   Antonym: Arrogant
    Say What? hyoo-mi-luh-tee   BOM 1

I might be a braggadocio but I'm allowed to flex when I run faster than a car down a residential street.

Absolutely Vocabulous — deduce   BOM 2

Using data from previous disruptions of daily life such as 911, big time power outages, transit strikes, etc, demographers **deduced** that January 2021 to March 2021 would have a 'mini baby boom.' Boy, were they right. Girls too.

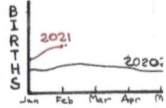

Feb 2021 - New Record
42 Boys   49 Girls

Every one smile for the Group Picture.

Group Picture March 2, 2021

deduce: arrive at by reasoning; draw a logical conclusion; follow the data
Synonym: Glean   Say What? dih-doos   Antonym: Disregard

©2020 AbVocab Publishing, Inc. www.facebook.com/abvocab www.abvocab.com AbVocab™ with SketchiToons®

Bedlam - Tawdry

Waking up after a long night in Vegas, Stuart made a shocking discovery. Apparently, in the midst of the bedlam the previous night he got some tawdry tattoo on his face. That tattoo will forever be a stigmata attached to that night.

Bedlam: a scene of uproar and confusion
  Synonym: Pandemonium   Antonym: Calm
  Say What? bed-luhm   BOM 2

Tawdry: showy but cheap and of poor quality
  Synonym: Tasteless   Antonym: Classy
  Say What? taw-dree   BOM 2

Ummm, wth is that on my face.

Stigmata - a mark of disgrace

Arbitary

The TSA airport security guard peppered the sweet old nun with questions. She was under orders to arbitrarily pick someone who looked harmless so the airport wouldn't appear culturally biased.

Arbitrary: based on random choice rather and opinion rather than reason or system
    Synonym: Random   Antonym: Discriminate
    Say What? aar-buh-treh-ree   BOM 2

Come on Sister, we know you have explosives under this tunic

Exemplary

Bananas, like most foods that taste like dookie, are great for you. They are exemplary as a work out food. They have vitamin C, are fat free, have anti-inflammatory benefits, help you heal faster & are full of potassium. So don't overthink it, just shove one down your throat if you have to. If you are dehydrated, nothing helps more.

Exemplary: serving as a desirable model
    Synonym: Ideal   Antonym: Unworthy
    Say What? ig-zem-pluh-ree   BOM 2

I may taste like dookie but I got the goods.

Apoplectic

Bam the Bear told Ron to make him look rough and rugged. Ron thought it would be funny to put his hair up in a cute bun. Bam became apoplectic and chased Ron out of the barbershop.

Apoplectic: overcome with anger
    Synonym: Indignant   Antonym: Happy
    Say What? ap-o-plec-tic   BOM 4

Absolutely Vocabulous negation

To underscore the concept and execution of **negation**, the English as a Second Language (ESL) teacher took the class on a trip to the cemetery.

negation: the contradiction or denial or opposite of something
Synonym:Contradiction   Say What?ni-gey-shuhn   Antonym:Similarity

©2020 AbVocab Publishing, Inc. www.facebook.com/abvocab   www.abvocab.com   AbVocab™ with SketchiToons®

Malice

Torpid the tortoise knew he would never beat Hasty the hare in a race. He knew the fable "The Tortoise & the Hare" was bs. He had seen hares beat tortoises over and over. Full of malice and hate, he decided to cheat.

Malice: the intention or desire to do evil
    Synonym: Animosity   Antonym: Kind
    Say What? ma-luhs   BOM 2

Bohemian-Vagabond

Broski the beach bum never had much desire to do anything other than smoke weed and surf. His parents finally kicked him out of the house when he turned 30. Now he lives a bohemian lifestyle, a vagabond who lives in his purple van, surfing & drawing caricatures of people on the beach for food & beer money.

Bohemian: a socially unconventional artsy person
   Synonym: Free Spirit   Antonym: Conformist
   Say What? bo-hee-mee-uhn   BOM 3

Vagabond: a person who wanders from place to place without a home or job
   Synonym: Vagrant   Antonym: Inhabitant
   Say What? vag-uh-bond   BOM 2

Browski the bohemian vagabond living by his own rules

"Bruh, this is the life"

Recluse

Ralph was always the life of the party. He had an extensive circle of friends & his phone & Facebook account were filled with hundreds of contacts. He was in great shape, worked out daily & had a full set of hair. But then…. he got married. Within 5 years his list of contacts dwindled to 5, his muscle had atrophied into flab, he became bald & a recluse who rarely ventured out of the house.

Recluse: a person who lives a solitary life avoids other people
   Synonym: Hermit   Antonym: Extrovert
   Say What? ruh-kloos   BOM 2

Before, Ralph was the man. After, he got married. Now he is a recluse with no friends.

Salient

The man said a few animals escaped from his house. He left out the most salient detail: they were all pythons!

Salient: most noticeable or important
   Synonym: Notable Antonym: Unimportant
   Say What? sey-lee-uhnt   BOM 3

Absolutely Vocabulous: nostalgia BOM 3

For younger people the idea of 'social distancing' is uncharted territory, but for some Baby Boomers, it brings feelings of remembrance and of **nostalgia** for the days of youthful dances and proms. Twerking definitely not allowed.

Hey! Lover Boy! 12 inches apart!

nostalgia: sentimental longing, wistful affection for past, typically happy times
Synonym: Reminiscence   Say What? no-stal-juh   Antonym: Bitter

©2020 AbVocab Publishing, Inc. www.facebook.com/abvocab   www.abvocab.com   AbVocab™ with SketchiToons®

Maxim

Probably a good **maxim** to live by would be to not mess with someone who has cauliflower ears. In that case, just give up and take the L.

Maxim: a short statement expressing a general truth
   Synonym: Aphorism   Antonym: Yarn
   Say What? maksem   BOM 2

Cauliflower Ear: an ear that has become thickened or deformed as a result of repeated blows, typically in boxing or wrestling

Don't know who this guy is but trust me, just take the L.

48

Anarchy

In the 1800's, the saloon towns of the wild west were hotbeds of lawlessness and anarchy. Gold prospectors were flooding to California and the Government offered free land to the West. Sounds great right? Well, you could just as easily get burned with syphilis from a prostitute as you could find gold. It was also 90% male and whenever you get that kind of sausage fest it tends to lead to all sorts of alpha-male macho stuff like duels & shootouts & bar fights.

Anarchy: state of disorder due to no authority
  Synonym: Disorder   Antonym: Harmony
  Say What? a-naar-kee   BOM 2

Duel at the Saloon. Predictable anarchy when you have a sausage fest

Sausage Fest - an event with all dudes

Veneer

If you are a bird, let me warn you: The Spider-tailed horned viper snake is not what it looks like, it is a veneer! Trust me. This Iranian snake's tail is shaped like a spider with thin 'legs' sticking out to lure you in. But once you go in to eat the spider, it will attack and kill you.

Veneer: to disguise someone or something's true nature with an attractive appearance
  Synonym: Pretense   Antonym: Reality
  Say What? vuh-neer   BOM 2

Noooo, it is a veneer! That snake is about to eat you!

Jingoism

Americans love how badass their military is. They think the cure to all problems is a bigger & better fighter jet or aircraft carrier. Those are nice, but maybe take some of that jingoism and re-direct it at preventing and fighting disease & repairing and improving our infrastructure, among other things. 'Murica!

Jingoism: extreme patriotism, especially in the form of aggressive or warlike foreign policy
  Synonym: Hawkish   Antonym: Dovish
  Say What? jing-goh-iz-uh m   BOM 3

I'm not sure what to do but let's just bomb it first, ask questions later. 'Murica!

lucrative

After a week of beratements and no reward, Jeff thought porta-potty cleaning would be more lucrative than trading stocks. He quit just after his training session showed what a bunch of shit he'd have to put up with. Bought new tie.

lucrative: producing a lot of profit or money
Synonym: Fruitful   Say What? loo-kruh-tiv   Antonym: Unprofitable

©2020 AbVocab Publishing, Inc. www.facebook.com/abvocab   www.abvocab.com   AbVocab™ with SketchiToons®

Aptitude

After seeing Reginae argue with a tree as a child, her parents knew that they would see her natural aptitude fully displayed in the courtroom as a high profile lawyer.

Aptitude: a natural ability to do something
    Synonym: Faculty   Antonym: Inability
    Say What? ap-ti-tood   BOM 2

Your argument is invalid tree!

Ennui-Lethargy-Dissolute

During the quarantine, the daily the couch potato ennui in Ted's life led to a re-emergence of bad habits. He gave up his routine of exercising & working hard. He woke up at noon & didn't shave. His self-control gave in to lethargy and dissolute behavior such as trolling internet porn & random chat rooms. He gained weight that he termed the 'quarantine 15' in memory of the freshman 15 he gained his first year in college.

Ennui: idleness from a lack of excitement
    Synonym: Languor   Antonym: Vigor
    Say What? aan-wee   BOM 3

Lethargic: lack of energy
    Synonym: Slothful   Antonym: Energetic
    Say What? luh-thaar-juhk   BOM 2

Dissolute: lax in morals
    Synonym: Indulgent   Antonym: Virtuous
    Say What? dis-uh-loot   BOM 2

"Guess I'll watch some trash on tv and then filter through pornhub"

Homily

The Noah's Ark homily teaches us a couple things other than not pissing off the big guy. Next time, we have to find a way of keeping the grizzly & polar bears from mating. We had damn Grolar bears all over the Ark last time. With 350,000 species of beetle, we need to find a better way of keeping them contained. We also had parasites that were all over the place & Noah ended up with some yeast infection.

Homily: a religious story
    Synonym: Sermon
    Say What? hom-uh-lee   BOM 3

Uggh, where are we going to put all of the beetles & Grolar Bears? We need a bigger boat.

ingenuity

With gyms closed because of COVID-19 concerns, Santa Fe strength and aerobics trainers showed their **ingenuity** and creativity to offer 'Drive To' classes satisfying the 'social distancing' requirements.

ingenuity: the quality of being clever, original, and inventive
Synonym: Resourcefulness Say What? in-juh-noo-itee Antonym: Inability

©2020 AbVocab Publishing, Inc. www.facebook.com/abvocab www.abvocab.com AbVocab™ with SketchiToons®

Parable

Jack and Jill is a very strange parable. Jack and Jill went up the hill to fetch a pail of water, Jack fell down and broke his crown and Jill came tumbling after. A couple lessons from this: Women should not follow behind men, especially stupid ass men like Jack. Also, wise females know that water does not run up hill.

Parable - a simple story used to illustrate a moral or spiritual lesson
 Synonym: Fable
 Say What? par-uh-buhl   BOM 2

Look at Jill following that stupid boy

Unscrupulous-Conspired

The unscrupulous real estate developer conspired with the crooked builder in a ploy to clump as many cheap, cookie cutter, pre-fab homes into the neighborhood as quickly as possible.

Unscrupulous: having or showing no moral principles
    Synonym: Shady   Antonym: Honest
    Say What? uhn-skroo-pyuh-luhs   BOM 2

Conspire: make secret plans commit an unlawful or harmful act
    Synonym: Collude   Antonym: Neglect
    Say What? kuhn-spai-ur   BOM 2

So let me get this straight. We are going to smash as many crap homes in that neighborhood as possible? Brilliant.

Vociferous

Donny, the vociferous leader of a scream style hard-core punk band comes from a middle class home with two loving parents. But nobody understands me he thought, and my dad is a real ball buster. I take out my rage in my music.

Vociferous: outspoken
    Synonym: Clamorous   Antonym: Quiet
    Say What? Vow-si-fr-uhs   BOM 2

Rage against the machine!

Pizzazz

We all know Muhammad Ali had plenty of pizzazz but what is often overlooked about his boxing was how fast his feet were. By the time you threw a punch, he was in a completely different place making you punch the air. The combination of his size, strength, nimble feet made him impossble to defeat.

Pizzazz: energy; flamboyance
    Synonym: Flair   Antonym: Boring
    Say What? puh-zaz   BOM 3

"Fly like a butterfly, sting like a bee"

Absolutely Vocabulous — emasculate

It took only two therapy sessions before James Soften realized that his feelings of **emasculation** went back to age six being constantly blocked taking the rock to the bucket against a younger and shorter neighbor. A girl no less.

"You're no Kobe! No Luka!"

emasculate: deprive a male of his masculine role or identity
Synonym: Devitalize   Say What? ih-mas-kyuh-leyt   Antonym: Invigorate

©2020 AbVocab Publishing, Inc. www.facebook.com/abvocab   www.abvocab.com   AbVocab™ with SketchiToons®

Paragon

Tom Brady is the paragon of the modern Quarterback. He is talented, has a great arm & wins super bowls, although to be honest, his wife is much better looking.

Paragon: a person or thing regarded as a perfect example of a particular quality

Synonym: Exemplar   Antonym: Worst
Say What? par-uh-gon   BOM 2

GISELE BÜNDCHEN
Definitely better looking than Tom

Inept-Nefarious

To casual observers, Kim Jong-Un comes across as the silly, inept leader of North Korea, aka the hermit kingdom. A deeper dive reveals a ruthless, nefarious mob boss who happened to be next in line in this revolting necrocracy in which his dead grandfather is still worshipped.

Inept: having or showing no skill; clumsy
    Synonym: Incompetent   Antonym: Able
    Say What? uh-nept   BOM 2

Nefarious: wicked or criminal action
    Synonym: Corrupt   Antonym: Honorable
    Say What? nuh-feh-ree-uhs   BOM 3

Necrocracy: a government that still operates under the rules of a former, dead leader

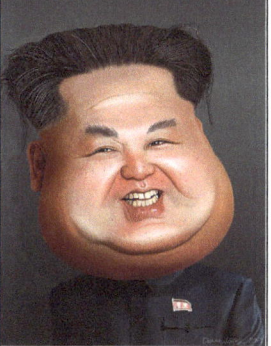

Kim Jong-Un: Test case for why hereditary dictatorships are bad.

Alienate-Premeditate

Sal the snowman was jealous about all of the attention that Ned was getting. All the kids wanted to play with him. His snow was soft & easy to use. Ned felt alienated. So he snapped. In an act of premeditation, he would steal the blowtorch, liquidate Sal, steal his hat & buttons & see if the kids would play with him then.

Alienate- to cause someone to feel isolated
    Synonym: Isolate   Antonym: Include
    Say What? eyl-yuh-neyt   BOM 2

Premeditate- to plan beforehand
    Synonym: Plan   Antonym: Impulsive
    Say What? pree-meh-duh-tei-tuhd   BOM 2

"Don't take it personal Ned but I need some attention too".

Diabolical

I know we are supposed to wear masks during this time but if you see someone wearing a diabolical, Hannibal Lector looking thing, run!

Diabolical: evil
    Synonym: Heinous   Antonym: Pleasant
    Say What? dai-uh-baa-li-kl   BOM 3

Absolutely Vocabulous: scatalogical BOM 4

Due to his hideous cologne, every one in the bar knew that Freddie Junior had made his weekly entrance. Being Absolutely Vocabulous, the ladies described this jerk vividly and without resorting to **scatalogical** references.

Schmuck! Twerp!
Doofus! Schlepper!
Cretin! Dipstick!
Miscreant! Dullard!
Wanker! Prat!
Sleazeball! Amadon!

scatalogical: obscenity, especially words or humor referring to exerement
Synonym: Bawdy   Say What? skuh-tol-uh-jee   Antonmy: Decent

©2020 AbVocab Publishing, Inc. www.facebook.com/abvocab   www.abvocab.com   AbVocab™ with SketchiToons®

Acrimonious

The high school soccer game became *acrimonious* when a player got slide tackled and no call was made. The player got in the referee's face and was issued a red card.

Acrimonious - angry and bitter
   Synonym: Rancorous   Antonym: Pleasant
   Say What? ak-ruh-moh-nee-uhs   BOM 3

Apartheid-Inauguration-Merit

Nelson Mandela has an amazing story. He ran away from home to escape arranged marriage. He had three children who died. Finally, he was thrown in prison for 20 years because he protested against the racist Apartheid system then ruling South Africa. His inauguration as President & numerous awards & prizes have been well merited.

Apartheid- racial segregation
    Synonym: Racism   Antonym: Inclusion
    Say What? uh-pahrt-hahyt   BOM 3

Inaugurate- to begin or introduce a system, policy, or period
    Synonym: Debut   Antonym: End
    Say What? in-aw-gyuh-reyt   BOM 3

Merit- to deserve or be worthy of something
    Synonym: Earned   Antonym: Undeserved
    Say What? mer-it   BOM 2

What a life this man led and is a true inspiration to all.

Unflappable

When Shawn Carter AKA "Jay-Z" started out, he couldn't get anyone to sign a record deal with him. He sold tapes out of the trunk of his car & went door to door trying to get his name out. Because of his unflappable attitude, he eventually became arguably the best rapper of all time.

Unflappable- showing determination when in a crisis
    Synonym: Imperturbable   Antonym: Fluster
    Say What? uhn-fla-puh-bl   BOM 3

"I will not lose, for even in defeat, there's a valuable lesson learned, so it evens up for me."

Irreconcilable

Tom & Katie were having a tough marriage. Their views on life, kids, money & politics were irreconcilable. They agreed to take up Karate to unleash some frustration and their marriage was saved.

Irreconcilable: points of view that are so different from each other that they cannot be made compatible

    Synonym: Incompatible   Antonym: Similar
    Say What? ih-rek-uhn-sahy-luh-buhl BOM 3

"I'm not even sure why we were so mad at each other honey"

Mantra-Contemplative

The meditating frog repeated the mantra "focus on the breath". This was easier said than done. The more he tried to be contemplative, the more he found that his brain was being bombarded with a tornado of thoughts making it hard to concentrate.

Mantra: a statement or slogan repeated frequently usually to aid in meditation

    Synonym: Chant   Antonym: Action
    Say What? man-truh   BOM 1

Contemplative: in prayer or meditation, inner vision that is transcendent of the intellect

    Synonym: Meditative   Antonym: Shallow
    Say What? kuhn-tem-pluh-tiv   BOM 3

"Focus on the breath, live in the present. Damn, why do I keep thinking of that party?"

Primp

My name is Bailey & the Westminister dog show is my special time. My glam squad spends hours & thousands of dollars to primp my absolutely fabulous Afghan coat so I can go destroy Dalia, the prissy Bichon Frise in the finals.

Primp: nitpick over minor flaws in one's hair

    Synonym: Preen   Antonym: Ignore
    Say What? primp   BOM 1

"I'm done getting primped, time to take on that snob Dalia"

Elixir-Panacea

Mushroom city was a magical place deep underground. The mushrooms contained a powerful exlir that would make the ogre's live forever and even fly. This panacea was hidden from the humans who lived above the earth's crust.

Elixir- a magical or medicinal potion
    Synonym: Medicine   Antonym: Poison
    Say What? ih-lik-ser   BOM 3

Panacea- a cure all; universal remedy; magical potion
    Synonym: Cure-all   Antonym: Disease
    Say What? pan-uh-see-uh   BOM 2

I hope the humans above never find us. We have the panacea!

Irascible-Chagrin

Dhalsim was a mild mannered, elastic limbed pacifist who only fought to raise money for his poor village. But to his chagrin, people were calling him washed up and old. This made him angry and irascible. Determined to prove to the doubters that he could still street fight, he whooped Ken's ass.

Irascible: having or showing a tendency to be easily angered
    Synonym: Cantankerous   Antonym: Happy
    Say What? ir-a-suh-bl   BOM 3

Chagrin: distressed or embarrassment at having failed or been humiliated
    Synonym: Dismay   Antonym: Delight
    Say What? shuh-grin   BOM 3

"My fire breath will destroy your fireball. Victory is to control yourself as well as control the opponent"

Desultory

Hank had just retired after 30 years as a homicide detective in his native Boston, MA. Being a cop was what he took pride in. For a while he made a desultory attempt to join the guys at the bar after their shift to drink beer & laugh but it wasn't the same. He felt like an outsider. He spends his days now reading suspenseful police books and watching the tube.

Desultory: lacking a plan, purpose, or enthusiasm

    Synonym: Tepid   Antonym: Purposeful
    Say What? des-uh l-tawr-ee   BOM 3

Extradite

The smelly cheese bandit from France stole 10,000 lbs of Limburger cheese from a cheese factory in Germany. When the Germans went to extradite him back to France they were unsure whether to shackle his hands or feet because they both smelled horrifically like cheese.

Extradite: hand over a person accused of a crime to the jurisdiction in which the crime was committed

    Synonym: Deliver   Antonym: Keep
    Say What? ek-struh-dahyt   BOM 3

Uh oh, they caught me cheese handed!

Plebeian

The plebeians stood around and ate jello shots & flossed Gangnam style in ancient Rome. Wait, no they didn't. That was me at the Toga party the other night.

Plebeian: belonging to the commoners of ancient Rome

    Synonym: Peasant   Antonym: Aristocratic
    Say What? pli-bee-uhn   BOM 3

Jello Shots, Roman Style!

Prestigious

How dumb are hereditary monarchies? Do we really need to give some people special status & prestige just because they happened to born in a certain family? Barf. It's a good thing that the King & Queen are just puppet leaders that don't really have any power. Voting people into office because of their character & ability is soooo much better.

Prestigious: inspiring respect and admiration; having high status
    Synonym: Exalted   Antonym: Ordinary
    Say What? pre-stij-uhs   BOM 3

Queen Elizabeth just happened to be born to the right family. Good thing we outgrew this.

Hegemony-Menacing

Russians have kept their worldwide hegemony on Vodka because the have nothing better to do than grow potatoes & stand around looking menacing in the cold.

Hegemony: dominance, especially by one country or social group over others
    Synonym: Power   Antonym: Inferior
    Say What? huh-jeh-muh-nee   BOM 4

Menacing: suggesting the presence of danger
    Synonym: Threatening   Antonym: Cordial
    Say What? men-is-ing   BOM 2

We vwill dominate Vodka Mardket. Need more potatoes.

Intrinsic

It appears that men were born with intrinsic qualities such as the need to be right even when they can see in real time evidence to the contrary, a language processing deficit & the inability to put the toilet seat down after they pee while women have instrinsic qualities such as making zero sense when they speak & the inability to put the toilet up after they pee.

Intrinsic- born with
    Synonym: Inherent   Antonym: Learned
    Say What? in-trin-sik   BOM 3

Nepotism

The banana republic dictator was accused of nepotism after he hired his son as secretary of defense, daughter as ambassador to France and his Labrador retriever as Secretary of Agriculture.

Nepotism: hiring people you know for a job they are not qualified for

    Synonym: Favoritism   Antonym: Fairness
    Say What? nep-uh-tiz-uhm   BOM 3

I'm the new Secretary of Agriculture. Kneel before me. The only food our country will produce will be Beef Jerky.

Pugilist

The Brazilian UFC champion Anderson Silva is arguably the best mixed martial arts pugilist of all time. With a lethal repertoire of raw talent, unparalleled athleticism & honed grappling and fighting techniques, Silva is the G.O.A.T. in the world of cage fighting.

Pugilist: a prizefighter

    Synonym: Fighter   Antonym: Pacifist
    Say What? pyoo-juh-luhst   BOM 3

GOAT of UFC

Prescient-Annex

In what might go down as the most prescient real estate deal of all time, Thomas Jefferson was able double the size of the United States by annexing all land west of the Mississippi River in the Louisiana Purchase. He did this for a paltry $15 Million which would cost over $1 Trillion dollars today!

Prescient: having or showing knowledge of events before they take place

    Synonym: Far Sighted   Antonym: Myopic
    Say What? presh-uhnt   BOM 3

Annex: attaching, uniting, or joining together in a physical sense

    Synonym: Consolidate   Antonym: Reduce
    Say What? an-eks   BOM 2

Thomas Jefferson annexed almost 1 million square miles of land!

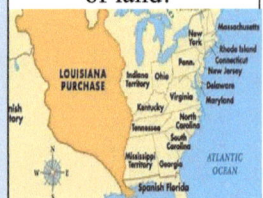

Debunk-Balderdash

It is high time to debunk this silly myth that if you shave your hair, it will grow back faster and thicker. It only appears that hair grows back thicker during the first cycle of hair growth. But if this were true, balding people could lessen their hair loss by just shaving more so their hair would keep growing faster and thicker. So, that theory is a bunch of 'bald'erdash, pun intended.

Debunk: to expose the falseness or hollowness of a myth, idea, or belief
    Synonym: Disprove   Antonym: Confirm
    Say What? dih-buhngk   BOM 2

Balderdash: senseless talk
    Synonym: Nonsense   Antonym: Wisdom
    Say What? bawl-der-dash   BOM 4

"I think if I just shave the top of my head it will grow back as thick as the hair near my ears"

Quagmire-Embellish

The Vietnam War was the quagmire of all quagmires. America was fighting an enemy it couldn't see in terrain it didn't know in a war it didn't understand. President Johnson embellished the threat of Communism by saying that it would spread like a disease thru the world if we didn't go to a jungle in South East Asia. History is full of these wtf moments.

Quagmire: a complex or hazardous situation
    Synonym: Disaster   Antonym: Ideal
    Say What? kwag-mahyuhr   BOM 3

Embellish: make a statement or story more interesting or entertaining by adding extra details, especially ones that are not true
    Synonym: Exaggerate Antonym: Downplay
    Say What? em-bel-ish   BOM 2

Vietnam was the mother of all Quagmires

Expeditiously-Squelch

The firemen and firewomen at fire station 20 were enjoying their balmy Saturday. There were ribs on the grill, music playing over the loudspeaker & a friendly game of outdoor volleyball going on. All of a sudden, out of nowhere, the alarm when off. The giant inferno was 15 blocks away. They expeditiously got into their fire trucks and took off. The ribs & volleyball could wait, they had a fire to squelch.

Expeditiously: with speed and efficiency
    Synonym: Urgently   Antonym: Casually
    Say What? ek-spuh-di-shuh-slee   BOM 3

Squelch: forcefully silence or suppress
    Synonym: Stymie   Antonym: Permit
    Say What? skwelch   BOM 2

Emergency at fire station 20. The fun in the sun will have to wait!

Infallible

The search for Colonel Sanders infallible Fried Chicken recipe continues. There have been several frauds claiming to have gotten hold of the 11 spices which make the chicken 'finger lickin good' but they turned out not to be the real thing. Sanders would rather die than give you his recipe but after eating all that chicken over the years, this may happen sooner rather than later.

Infallible: incapable of making mistakes or being wrong
    Synonym: Unerring   Antonym: Flawed
    Say What? in-fal-uh-buhl   BOM 2

You will never ascertain the secret recipe for my finger lickin good fried chicken!

Partisan

Partisan liberals and conservatives spend hours a day seeking approval and affirmation from liked minded primates in their tiny echo chamber on the internet ensuring they won't have to encounter ideas that are different from what they believe and will guarantee that they won't ever reach the full height of their cognitive capacity. Bipartisanship is a thing of the past.

Partisan: A strong supporter of a party or cause
    Synonym: Biased   Antonym: Open Minded
    Say What? pahr-tuh-zuhn   BOM 2

Oxymoron

See how many oxymorons there are in this paragraph (Hint: There are 10)

During the Great Depression, it got pretty ugly. People were clearly confused thinking it was just a minor crisis. How could you act naturally when original copies show people ran out of jumbo shrimp. The only choice was for everyone to be alone together for almost exactly 10 years.

Oxymoron- a figure of speech in which apparently contradictory terms appear in conjunction
    Synonym: Contradiction   Antonym: Same
    Say What? ok-si-mawr-on   BOM 2

Dystopia

After being infected by parasites, humans turned into Zombies and wandered around in a dystopian wasteland desert.

Dystopia: an post-apocalypic imagined state
    Synonym: Apocalypse   Antonym: Utopian
    Say What? dis-toh-pee-uh   BOM 3

Personification-Anthropomorphic

'Shrek' is an animated movie about a Scottish ogre named shrek. "I'm An Ogre! You Know, 'Grab Your Torch And Pitchforks!' Doesn't That Bother You?" The fable uses personification and anthropomorphic qualities. The donkey saying "parfaits are delicious" & princess Fiona changing from human form to ogre are examples of this.

Personification: a person, animal, or object regarded as representing or embodying a quality, concept, or thing
    Synonym: Role   Antonym: Normal
    Say What? per-son-uh-fi-key-shuhn   BOM 3

Anthropomorphic: human characteristics or behavior to a god, animal, or object
    Synonym: Human Antonym: Zoomorphism
    Say What? an-thruh-puh-mawr-fik   BOM 4

Mastication-Trope

The biology teacher was giving a presentation about the Digestive System. When he said "digestion starts with mastication" the immature teenage boy yelled out the trope "that's what she said".

Masticate: to chew food
Synonym: Chew   Antonym: Swallow
Say What? mas-ti-keyt   BOM 3
Trope: an idea or device that repeatedly appears
    Synonym: Cliché   Antonym: Original
    Say What? trohp   BOM 3

Rhetoric-Harangue

Marshall Mathers AKA Eminem is one of the most rhetorically gifted rappers of all time. His no hold barred, fire spittin', scathing harangues about life and relationships leave the listener energized. Whether performing a cappella or with a beat, Slim Shady will tell you how he feels.

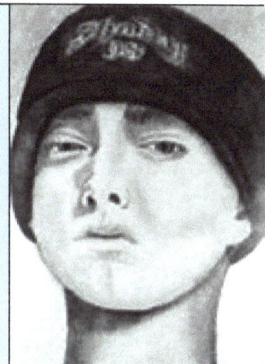

"I'm not a player just a ill rhyme sayer that'll spray an Aerosol can up in the ozone layer"

Rhetoric: language designed to have a persuasive or impressive effect on its audience
    Synonym: Bombast   Antonym: Quiet
    Say What? reh-tr-uhk   BOM 2

Harangue: a lengthy and aggressive speech
    Synonym: Tirade   Antonym: Eulogy
    Say What? hr-ang   BOM 3

Circumlocution

When confronted by his mom, the teenager used circumlocution to try to talk around the fact that he went to a party. "Well, um, what had happened was, I was at this guys house and we were talking and having a good time, more of a get together really."

Circumlocution: the use of many words where fewer would do, especially in a deliberate attempt to be vague or evasive
    Synonym: Evasive   Antonym: Honest
    Say What? surkuhm-loh-kyooshuhn BOM 3

Contort

Chad was snow boarding down a black diamond slope when he heard the rumbling of an avalanche behind him. He tried to contort his body but couldn't avoid the punishing snow. This was not good.

Contort: twist or bend out of the normal shape
    Synonym: Disfigure   Antonym: Straighten
    Say What? kuhn-tawrt   BOM 2

Taciturn-Choleric

Melinda was trying to explain her day to Craig when she noticed he wasn't listening to a damn thing she was saying. His taciturn responses just made her even more choleric. "You aren't listening to anything are you? You just sit there a watch sports." "Yes dear". "Ugghh, you make me want to pull out my hair!"

Taciturn: reserved or uncommunicative
    Synonym: Terse   Antonym: Expansive
    Say What? tas-i-turn   BOM 3

Choleric: bad-tempered or irritable
    Synonym: Irascible Antonym: Cheerful
    Say What? kol-er-ik   BOM 3

Bewilder

Jim was perusing some books at the local library when out of nowhere a crazy old man walked up to him and told him he was going to pay for what he did. Jim was bewildered as he had no clue what the man was talking about.

Bewilder: a feeling of being perplexed and confused
    Synonym: Mystify   Antonym: Clarify
    Say What? buh-wil-dr   BOM 2

Abject

Melissa was talked into kid sitting her nephews Luke & Brock. It was abject misery. They terrorized the house, didn't follow any rules and put picture of her on Instagram. "I don't care how much I get paid, never again!"

Abject: a person without pride or dignity; also, something bad experienced to the maximum degree
    Synonym: Hopeless   Antonym: Excellent
    Say What? ab-jekt   BOM 2

Irrevocable

Clem the Chameleon saw what he thought was a big juicy fly to snack on. He shot out his tongue and gobbled up, oh wait that's not a fly. It's a dynamite stick! This decision was now irrevocable and would be his last.

Irrevocable: not able to be changed, reversed, or recovered; final
    Synonym: Immutable   Antonym: Alterable
    Say What? ih-rev-uh-kuh-buhl   BOM 3

Catatonic

The cat Cara had a tough day at work. As soon as she got home, she engorged herself with junk food, cigarrettes & beer until she was in a catatonic stupor. She didn't move until the next day.

Catatonic: of or in an immobile or unresponsive state
    Synonym: Oblivious   Antonym: Lucid
    Say What? kat-uh-ton-ik   BOM 3

Inexorable

Todd's car broke down next to an open field. When he got out of the car, a crazy looking rabid dog approached. He said "good doggie" but it was too late. It was impossible to resist the dog's inexorable desire to attack.

Inexorable: impossible to stop or prevent
    Synonym: Pitiless   Antonym: Remorse
    Say What? in-ek-ser-uh-buhl   BOM 3

Venerate

Wouldn't it be cool if we venerated doctors to the same degree we do famous celebrities, movie stars & musicians?

Venerate: regard with great respect
    Synonym: Revere   Antonym: Condemn
    Say What? veh-nr-eit   BOM 2

Confluence

A tornado is formed from a confluence of warm and humid air colliding with cold and dry air. This creates an updraft that starts to rotate if winds vary sharply in speed.

Confluence: the act or process of merging
    Synonym: Convergence Antonym: Division
    Say What? kon-floo-uhns   BOM 3

Flippant

Jeff was told repeatedly by friends, family and mechanics that he should get his oil changed every 3000-5000 miles. He blew them off in a flippant tone saying "this car is so strong it doesn't need no oil change". His car thought otherwise.

Flippant: to take serious matter lightly
    Synonym: Frivolous   Antonym: Serious
    Say What? fli-pnt   BOM 3

Permeable

Ralph was great at scoring but a scrub as a Goalie. His defense was extra permeable on Saturday when he gave up 15 goals.

Permeable: able to pass through
    Synonym: Porous   Antonym: Inpenetrable
    Say What? pur-mee-uh-buhl   BOM 3

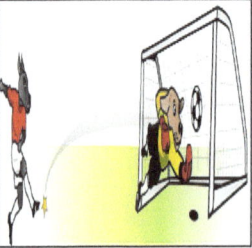

Idiosyncratic

Bats certainly have an idiosyncratic way of sleeping. So why do they sleep upside down? Well, they can avoid predators easier & reach flight faster. Also, because they only weigh a few ounces they don't have to worry about blood flowing from gravity. Pretty cool!

Idiosyncratic: a distinctive or peculiar feature or characteristic of a place or thing
    Synonym: Quirky   Antonym: Typical
    Say What? id-ee-oh-sin-krat-ik   BOM 3

Pollyanna-Cassandra

As the Corona Virus blazed its way through the country, sisters Pollyanna & Cassandra couldn't have reacted more differently. Cassandra spent a week building an underground bunker & stocking up on canned goods. Pollyanna on the other hand flouted the lockdown & headed to the beach.

Pollyanna: an excessively optimistic person
    Synonym: Optimist   Antonym: Pessimist
    Say What? pol-ee-an-uh   BOM 3

Cassandra: one who predicts disaster
    Synonym: Worrywort   Antonym: Optimist
    Say What? kuh-san-druh   BOM 3

Cassandra

Pollyanna

Ruminate-Sartorial

The little girl had dreams of being a fashion designer with sartorial splendor. She ruminated about the possibilities of designing clothes for celebrities in Hollywood.

Ruminate: to think about something deeply
    Synonym: Cogitate   Antonym: Forget
    Say What? roo-muh-neyt   BOM 3

Sartorial: relating to tailoring, clothes, or style
    Synonym: Stylish   Antonym: Frumpy
    Say What? saar-taw-ree-uhl   BOM 3

One day my clothes will be worn by all the stars.

Continuity

After the passing of Bob Marley, a new Reggae band had to pick up the mantle. Rasta Mouse was the obvious choice with their continuity of steel drums, staccato beats, dredlock rasta creating the sound of Jamaica.

Continuity: cohesion & consistency among various elements

    Synonym: Cohesion   Antonym: Discord
    Say What? kon-tn-oo-itee   BOM 3

Extirpate

The merry gang of white blood cells went by the moniker 'will be courageous' and fought their hearts out for Dave. Dave unfortunately was in terrible health from smoking, alcohol use, lack of exercise & poor hygiene. Alas, the white blood cells including noble neurophil, marvelous monocyte and limber lymphocyte couldn't save Dave. In their final battle against germs in his body, the WBC's got extirpated and completely destroyed.

Extirpate: root out and destroy completely

    Synonym: Conquer   Antonym: Fix
    Say What? ek-ster-peyt   BOM 3

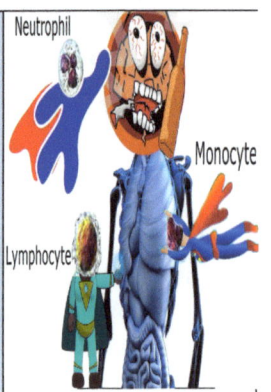

WBC's were courageous but got extirpated

Relegate-Steadfast

Tanya used to work at a local salon. She was relegated to working long hours. Her bosses talked down to her and her wages were unlivable. She said "flip this" and opened up her own salon. Because she was steadfast in the face of adversity, her salon is now thriving.

Relegate: to dismiss to an inferior position

    Synonym: Downgrade   Antonym: Promote
    Say What? rel-i-geyt   BOM 2

Steadfast: resolutely firm and unwavering

    Synonym: Resolute   Antonym: Waver
    Say What? sted-fast   BOM 2

Come get your style on at Tanya's Tousled Tresses

Discombobulate

Nancy was in over her head. She had to deal with animals, babies & a house to clean. She felt discombobulated and confused. Now how do I iron this shirt, breast-feed this baby, talk to the insurance company and walk this dog.

Discombobulate: confused and disoriented
   Synonym: Flustered   Antonym: Composed
   Say What? dis-kuhm-bob-yuh-leyt   BOM 3

Clairvoyant

The crazy astrologist stubbornly insisted she was clairvoyant. A person's personality obviously would be correlated with the position of the planets when they were born she thought. No doubt she also probably believes in alchemy, 4 humors of the body, witchcraft & unicorns.

Clairvoyant: can see the future; prescient
   Synonym: Prophetic   Antonym: Myopic
   Say What? klair-voi-uhnt   BOM 3

Sanctimonious

The sanctimonious cat stared at the dog itching fleas and said "you are an ugly, flea infested, disgusting mutt, why don't you go try to stop a car by running under its tires."

Sanctimonious: act morally superior to others
   Synonym: Self-Righteous   Antonym:Meek
   Say What? sangk-tuh-mow-neeuhs   BOM 3

Bacchanalian

Ahmed, who was from Pakistan, was excited to finally go to Mecca on his Hajj. He and his pal from a local mosque started out plodding thru Afghanistan, next ate Persian ice cream in Iran, and finally bought some new Kanye's Yeezy's at a Bazaar in Iraq. They hit up a Halal nightclub in Saudi Arabia and it turned into a bacchanalian throw-down. The expedition was now complete.

Bacchanalian: drunken revelry
    Synonym: Carouse   Antonym: Abstainer
    Say What? bak-uh-ney-lee-uhn   BOM 4

Hajj: the muslim pilgrimage to Mecca

Omen

Tim was bald which was a bad omen for his future kids. Before marrying Kim, he needed to check out his father-in-law Ike's dome at the local bakery to ensure his son would be predisposed to flowing locks. Bad news, kids are screwed.

Omen: an event indicating future success
    Synonym: Portent   Antonym: Conclusion
    Say What? oh-muhn   BOM 2

"Ah Hell, Ike is Bald"

Impressionable

The older goats were nothing but trouble. They were always leaving trash scattered around, eating the plants & flowers, smashing pumkins & causing mischief not realizing they were passing on these bad habits to the impressionable baby goats.

Impressionable: easily influenced
    Synonym: Susceptible   Antonym: Proud
    Say What? im-presh-uh-nuh-buhl   BOM 3

"Guess we're supposed to eat that trash?"

Riveting

The parents mistakenly thought their baby Jazmine was riveted by the toys but she was actually irritated when she realized they were the same 8 toys every day. "This is getting boring, I expected more from you guys, change the toys, dammit."

Riveting- completely compelling & engrossing
    Synonym: Captivating   Antonym: Boring
    Say What? ri-vuh-tuhng   BOM 2

"Same 8 toys? Definitely not riveted here."

Poignant

After years of fishing, Jake mysteriously became poignant one day watching the bass caught on the hook desperately flip for Oxygen. He wondered if the fish was suffering.

Poignant: evoking emotions
    Synonym: Sentimental   Antonym: Callous
    Say What? poy-nynt   BOM 2

"Oh, I'll just throw this one back."

Melancholy

The house cat who had never stepped foot outside before felt a tinge of melancholy staring out the window at the squirrels that he thought were taunting him. "I'm not as dumb as a dog so I won't bark but just know I'll kill you squirrels if I get a chance."

Melancholy: a feeling of sadness
    Synonym: Gloomy   Antonym: Euphoric
    Say What? meh-luhn-kaa-lee   BOM 2

Maudlin

Usually after a couple glasses of red wine, the woman became maudlin looking at pictures of her children when they were younger & now out of the house for the first time. After this fleeting moment, she went back to feeling euphoric that they were finally gone!

Maudlin: tearfully sentimental
    Synonym: Mawkish   Antonym: Euphoric
    Say What? maad-luhn   BOM 3

"Not maudlin no mo' Time for mom to finally have some fun!"

Perfidious

Most people know that the female praying mantis perfidiously bites the head off the male during mating. I'm curious if the male knows this is going to happen, but still does it anyway.

Perfidious: deceitful and untrustworthy
    Synonym: Deceitful   Antonym: Loyal
    Say What? pr-fi-dee-uhs   BOM 3

"It's Still Worth It"

Confound

Jessamine became so confounded when her boyfriend Bernard took out the trash and recycling without being nagged that she completely lost it. "You never take out the trash. The last time you did was after you called me fat. What did you do this time?"

Confound: cause surprise or confusion in someone, especially by acting against their expectations
    Synonym: Astonish   Antonym: Expect
    Say What? kon-found   BOM 3

"What the hell did u do this time Bernard?"

Erudite-Savant

Elon Musk will go down as one of the greatest minds of the 21st Century. This erudite, savant engineer has a passion for robotics, electric vehicles, solar panels & brain machine interfaces. And he invented Paypal. Oh and he builds rockets when he isn't busy with Tesla.

Erudite: a learned person
    Synonym: Brainy   Antonym: Ignorant
    Say What? eh-ruh-dait   BOM 3

Savant: a genius
    Synonym: Genius   Antonym: Dullard
    Say What? sa-vahnt   BOM 2

Homophone

The soul singing fish was not the sole singer in the band. As a band they were so bad that fleas listening had to flee town. No one wanted to pay a cent especially after giving off that fish scent. I pray they never come back in town or they will become prey to the angry audience. They should be singing under a dam with all of that damn racket.

Homophone - each of two or more words spelled differently but pronounced the same
    Say What? hom-uh-fohn   BOM 2

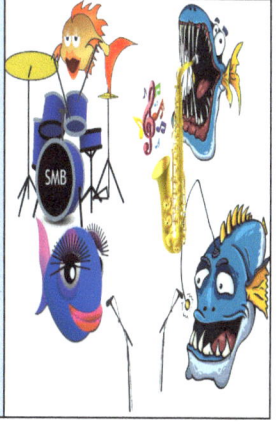

Vapid

Ian was fascinated by black holes in outer space & other astronomical explosions but always ended up having vapid conversations with friends about the weather.

Vapid: offering nothing that is stimulating
    Synonym: Boring   Antonym: Exciting
    Say What? va-puhd   BOM 3

"Would rather talk about these cool things"

Unparalleled

Milky Way chocolate bars are the GOAT. The creamy chocolate, smooth caramel & fluffy nougat make it unparalleled in the candy universe. Three musketeers misses the mark because the nougat is not fluffy enough and it didn't even have the courtesy of having caramel!

Unparalleled: having no equal
    Synonym: Incomparable   Antonym: Usual
    Say What? uhn-par-uh-leld   BOM 3
GOAT: Greatest of All Time

Candy Bar GOAT

Won't find any fluffy nougat problems here

Extricate-Exodus

When the mega tsunami started toppling buildings with ease, it was impossible for people to extricate themselves from this rogue wave. A mass exodus ensued but it was too late.

Extricate: free someone from a difficulty
    Synonym: Free   Antonym: Entangle
    Say What? ek-stri-keyt   BOM 3
Exodus: a mass departure of people
    Synonym: Evacuation   Antonym: Arrival
    Say What? ek-suh-duhs   BOM 2

Keen

Wolverine & deadpool hate each other. They have very similar in abilities & Deadpool even has some of Wolverine's DNA. They both have a regenerative healing factor. Wolverine has keen animal senses with 3 retractable claws. Deadpool is a lethal mercenary assassin with pain insensitivity & martial arts prowess. They met up to settle the score once and for all.

Keen: highly developed
    Synonym: Astute   Antonym: Dull
    Say What? keen   BOM 1

Remember, you are intelligent, erudite, imaginative, perceptive, sagacious, resourceful, inquisitive, discerning & knowledgeable.

You are going to Crush that Test!

Congratulations! You are going to do great!

Vocabulous Throwdown is a:

An *Absolutely Vocabulous*™ Production

Purchase Vocabulous Throwdown Volume 1 at Amazon.com to get the entire vocabulous experience

Vocabulary Words for Book (Alphabetical)

Abject: a person without pride or dignity; also, something bad experienced to the maximum degree
Abscond: leave hurriedly to avoid detection
Acrimonious- angry and bitter
Admonition: to give a warning
Aerobic: requiring oxygen
Alienate- to cause someone to feel isolated
Alleviate: make a problem less severe
Ambivalent: mixed feelings about something
Anarchy: state of disorder due to no authority
Annex: attaching, uniting, or joining together in a physical sense
Anthropocentric: regarding humankind as the most important
Anthropomorphic: human characteristics or behavior to a god, animal, or object
Apartheid- racial segregation
Apoplectic: overcome with anger
Aptitude: a natural ability to do something
Arbitrary: based on random choice and opinion not reason
Artisan: a worker in a skilled trade
Assuage: to make an unpleasant feeling less intense
Attenuate: to reduce force, effect, or value
Auspicious: conducive to success; favorable
Bacchanalian: drunken revelry
Balderdash: senseless talk
Balkanize: divide into smaller hostile groups
Bask: lie exposed to warmth from the sun
Bedlam: a scene of uproar and confusion
Belie: a fake appearance
Belligerent: hostile & aggressive
Bewilder: a feeling of being perplexed and confused
Bohemian: a socially unconventional artsy person
Boisterous: noisy, energetic, and cheerful
Braggadocio: boastful or arrogant
Bustling: full of activity
Cantankerous: bad-tempered; argumentative
Capitulate- cease to resist an opponent or an unwelcome demand
Carrion: the decaying flesh of dead animals
Cassandra: one who predicts disaster
Catatonic: of or in an immobile or unresponsive state

Cattywumpus: skewed, sideways or out of alignment
Chagrin: embarrassment at having failed or been humiliated
Cherubic: having childlike innocence
Chimera: a horrible or unreal creature of the imagination
Choleric: bad-tempered or irritable
Circumlocution: the use of many words where fewer would do, especially in a deliberate attempt to be vague or evasive
Clairvoyant: can see the future; prescient
Confluence: the act or process of merging
Confound: cause surprise or confusion in someone
Conscience: an inner feeling acting as a moral guide
Conspire: make secret plans commit an unlawful or harmful act
Contaminate- make something impure by exposure to a poisonous or polluting substance
Contemplative: in prayer or meditation, inner vision that is transcendent of the intellect
Contentious: causing an argument
Continuity: cohesion & consistency among various elements
Contort: twist or bend out of the normal shape
Covet: yearn to possess or have something
Debacle: a huge failure
Debunk: to expose the falseness or hollowness of an idea
Deduce: arrive at by reasoning; draw a logical conclusion
Despondent: in low spirits from loss of hope or courage
Desultory: lacking a plan, purpose, or enthusiasm
Diabolical: evil
Discombobulate: confused and disoriented
Disillusioned: disappointed in someone or something that one discovers to be less good than one had believed
Dissolute: lax in morals
Doctrinaire: impose doctrine but not practical
Dystopia: an post-apocalypic imagined state
Ecstasy: an overwhelming feeling of great happiness or excitement
Elixir- a magical or medicinal potion
Emasculate: deprive a male of his masculine role or identity
Embellish: make a statement or story more entertaining by adding extra details, especially ones that are not true
Encapsulate: express the essential features of something succinctly
Encroach: intrude on a person's territory
Engorge- eat to excess
Ennui: idleness from a lack of excitement

Enthrall: to capture the fascinated attention of
Erudite: a learned person
Exculpate: to show that someone is not guilty of wrongdoing
Exemplary: serving as a desirable model
Exodus: a mass departure of people
Expeditiously: with speed and efficiency
Extirpate: root out and destroy completely
Extradite: hand over a person accused of a crime to the jurisdiction in which the crime was committed
Extricate: free someone from a difficulty
Fastidious: attentive to accuracy & detail
Favela- a shantytown located within Brazil
Fiasco- a thing that is a complete failure, especially in a ludicrous or humiliating way
Flippant: to take serious matter lightly
Fossil Evidence: dating used to determine a fossils age
Freewheeling: characterized by a disregard for rules or conventions
Frigid: very cold in temperature
Gene: a unit of heredity which is transferred from a parent to offspring and is held to determine some characteristic of the offspring
Harangue: a lengthy and aggressive speech
Hegemony: dominance, especially by one country or social group over others
Homily: a religious story
Homophone- each of two or more words spelled differently but pronounced the same
Hubris: excessive self-pride
Humility: a low view of one's own importance
Idiosyncratic: a distinctive or peculiar feature or characteristic of a place or thing
Illicit: something against the law
Illustrious: respected, and admired for past achievements
Immortalized: confer enduring fame upon
Impetuous: acting quickly without thought
Impressionable: easily influenced
Impropriety: improper language, behavior, or character
Inaugurate- to begin or introduce a system, policy, or period
Incursion- sudden or brief invasion
Indefatigable: a person persisting tirelessly
Industrious: diligent and hard working
Immortalized: confer enduring fame upon

Impetuous: acting quickly without thought
Impressionable: easily influenced
Impropriety: improper language, behavior, or character
Inaugurate- to begin or introduce a system, policy, or period
Incursion- sudden or brief invasion
Indefatigable: a person persisting tirelessly
Industrious: diligent and hard working
Inept: having or showing no skill; clumsy
Inexorable: impossible to stop or prevent
Infallible: incapable of making mistakes or being wrong
Infant Mortality- the death of children under the age of 1 year
Infiltrate- enter a place to secretly to acquire information
Ingenuity: the quality of being clever, original and inventive
Inimical: intending to obstruct or harm
Insatiable: a desire impossible to satisfy
Intricate: very complicated or detailed
Intrinsic- born with
Irascible: having or showing a tendency to be easily angered
Irony: when actions have an effect exactly opposite from what is intended
Irreconcilable: points of view that are so different from each other that they cannot be made compatible
Irrevocable: not able to be changed, reversed, or recovered; final
Jarring: incongruous in a striking way
Jingoism: extreme patriotism, especially in the form of aggressive or warlike foreign policy
Keen: highly developed
Lethargic: lack of energy
Libertarian- one who seeks to maximize political freedom
Lionize: celebrate
Literal: taking words precisely as they are; no metaphor or allegory
Lucrative: producing a lot of profit or money
Lurid: vividly shocking especially explicit details of crime or sex
Malevolent: having a wish to do evil to others
Malice: the intention or desire to do evil
Mantra: a statement or slogan repeated frequently usually to aid in meditation
Masticate: to chew food
Maudlin: tearfully sentimental
Maxim: a short statement expressing a general truth
Melancholy: a feeling of sadness

Menacing: suggesting the presence of danger
Menagerie: a strange or diverse collection of people or things
Merit- to deserve or be worthy of something
Mythical: characteristic of myths or folk tales
Nadir: the lowest point in fortunes
Necrocracy: a government that still operates under the rules of a former, dead leader
Nefarious: wicked or criminal action
Negation: the contradiction or denial or opposite of something
Nepotism: hiring people you know for a job they are not qualified for
Nonchalant: appearing casually relaxed
Nostalgia: sentimental longing or wistful affection of the past, typically for a happy place or time with personal connections
Notorious: famous for bad reasons
Novice: a person new to or inexperienced in a field or situation
Obfuscate: render obscure, unclear, or unintelligible; becloud
Occlude- obstruct an opening or passage
Olfactory: relating to the sense of smell
Omen: an event indicating future success
Opiate: medicine used for pain relief
Ostensible: appearing to be true
Overzealous: overly devoted to pursuit of a cause or objective
Oxymoron- a figure of speech in which apparently contradictory terms appear in conjunction
Panacea- a cure all; universal remedy; magical potion
Parable- a simple story used to illustrate a moral or spiritual lesson
Paragon: a person or thing regarded as a perfect example of a particular quality
Partisan: A strong supporter of a party or cause
Pedantic: concerned with minor details
Perfidious: deceitful and untrustworthy
Permeable: able to pass through
Personification: a person, animal, or object regarded as representing or embodying a quality, concept, or thing
Pertinacious- holding firmly to a course of action
Photosynthesis: trees and plants use energy from sunlight and C02 from the air to make the food they need to live and grow
Pizzazz: energy; flamboyance
Platitude: an unoriginal & overused saying
Plebeian: belonging to the commoners of ancient Rome
Plethora: a large or excessive amount of something

Poignant: evoking emotions
Pollyanna: an excessively optimistic person
Precarious: not securely held or in position; dangerously likely to fall or collapse; lack of stability or uncertain situation
Premeditate- to plan beforehand
Prescient: having or showing knowledge of events before they take place
Prestigious: inspiring respect and admiration; having high status
Primp: nitpick over minor flaws in one's hair
Pristine: in its original condition
Probity: having strong moral principles
Propaganda: information that is designed to mislead or persuade
Prurient: excessive interest in sexual matters
Pugilist: a prizefighter
Pugnacious: eager or quick to argue or fight
Pun: a joke exploiting the different possible meanings of a word
Quagmire: a complex or hazardous situation
Quaker: a member of the Religious Society of Friends, a Christian movement devoted to peaceful principles
Quandary: state of uncertainty over what to do next in a difficult situation
Quid Pro Quo: a favor or advantage granted with something expected in return
Rarified: exlusive, rare & special ability
Recluse: a person who lives a solitary life avoids other people
Relegate: to dismiss to an inferior position
Renowned: known by many people
Resolute: admirably purposeful & determined
Retribution: punishment as vengeance for a wrong or criminal act
Revel: take pleasure in
Reverberate: vibrate in sound
Reverie: pleasantly lost in one's thoughts
Rhetoric: language designed to have a persuasive or impressive effect on its audience
Riveting- completely compelling & engrossing
Ruminate: to think about something deeply
Salient: most noticeable or important
Sanctimonious: act morally superior to others
Sartorial: relating to tailoring, clothes, or style
Savant: a genius
Self-Deprecating- overly modest or critical of oneself, especially with humor

Simile: comparison using like or as
Skeptical: not easily convinced; having doubts
Smolder: to burn slowly with smoke
Sordid- dirty or squalid
Squalid: a place extremely dirty and unpleasant, especially as a result of neglect
Squelch: forcefully silence or suppress
Staunch: loyal and committed in attitude
Steadfast: resolutely firm and unwavering
Stigmata- a mark of disgrace
Suffrage- the right to vote
Taciturn: reserved or uncommunicative
Tantalize: torment or tease someone with something that is unobtainable
Tawdry: showy but cheap and of poor quality
Tenacious: not readily relinquishing a position or principle
Throng- a large, densely packed crowd of people
Totalitarian: relating to a system of government that is centralized and dictatorial
Tremulous: shaking or quivering slightly
Tribalism: behavior and attitudes that stem from strong loyalty to one's own tribe or social group
Trope: an idea or device that repeatedly appears
Tundra- a vast, flat, treeless Arctic region in which the subsoil is permanently frozen
Unorthodox: contrary to what is usual, traditional, or accepted
Unparalleled: having no equal
Unscathed: without suffering any harm
Unscrupulous: having or showing no moral principles
Vagabond: a person who wanders from place to place without a home or job
Vapid: offering nothing that is stimulating
Veneer: to disguise someone or something's true nature with an attractive appearance
Venerate: regard with great respect
Vociferous: outspoken
Wet Market: a market selling fresh meat, fish, produce, and other perishable goods

Related Words

Abject: wretched, hopeless, absolute, contemptible, dishonorable, base
Abscond: depart, vanish, vamoose, flee, escape, skedaddle, bolt, split
Acrimonious: belligerent, cranky, testy, churlish, rancorous, petulant
Admonition: caution, warning, counsel, advice, apprisal, rebuke, scold
Aerobic: cardiorespiratory, oxygen intake, old lady workout, exercise
Alienate: ostracize, estrange, divide, disunite, isolate, disaffect, part
Alleviate: allay, assuage, mitigate, pacify, ease, modulate, ameliorate
Ambivalent: unsure, waver, vacillate, mixed, debatable, of two minds
Anarchy: lawless, chaos, confusion, disorder, cluster*uck, unrest
Annex: addition, extension, addendum, appendix, supplement, adjoin
Anodyne: anesthetic, narcotic, sedative, innocuous, bland, inoffensive
Anthropocentric: homocentric, bodily, corporeal, physical, hubris
Anthropomorphic: humanlike, anthropoid, manlike, humanoid
Apartheid: racial segregation, discrimination, separation, bigotry
Apoplectic: furious, irate, enraged, infuriated, paroxysm, exasperated
Aptitude: predilection, propensity, inclination, disposition, proclivity
Arbitrary: whimsical, capricious, random, inconsistent, offhand
Artisan: craftsperson, master, builder, carpenter, work with hands
Assuage: soothe, relieve, allay, alleviate, appease, placate, lessen
Attenuate: weaken, constrict, debilitate, vitiate, cripple, abate, deflate
Auspicious: favorable, encouraging, advantageous, promising, rosy
Bacchanalian: alcoholic, lush, wino, tippler, merrymaker, debauchee
Balderdash: nonsense, poppycock, drivel, bunk, twaddle, piffle
Balkanize: separate, split, carve up, divide, dislocate, disjoin, detach
Bask: laze, loll, lounge, relax, sunbathe, indulge, revel, wallow
Bedlam: chaos, clamor, commotion, pandemonium, uproar, hubbub
Belligerent: argumentative, ornery, cantankerous, contentious
Bewilder: confuse, baffle, befuddle, confound, fluster, mystify, addle
Bohemian: nonconformist, free spirit, beatnik, hippie, gypsy, artist
Boisterous: noisy, clamorous, rambunctious, rowdy, uproarious, loud
Braggadocio: braggart, blowhard, show-off, windbag, blusterer
Bungle: blunder, botch, err, flub, miscalculate, muff, mishandle, mar
Bustling: commotion, clamor, flurry, excitement, hubbub, rumpus
Capitulate: concede, surrender, yield, fold, submit, succumb, relent
Carrion: decaying flesh, roadkill, body, corpse, remains, rot, skull
Cassandra: pessimist, worrywart, doomsayer, kill-joy, party pooper
Catatonic: unaware, comatose, confused, disoriented, paralyzed
Chagrin: displeasure, annoyance, dismay, frustration, irritation
Cherubic: angelic, adorable, childlike, cute, innocent, sweet, babyish

Chimera: dream, fantasy, hallucination, specter, figment, mirage
Choleric: irritable, irascible, peevish, cantankerous, grouchy, angry
Circumlocution: wordiness, roundabout, discursiveness, indirectness
Clairvoyant: prescient, perceptive, visionary, prophetic, telepathic
Confluence: assemblage, convergence, conflux, concurrence
Confound: confuse, amaze, astonish, dumfound, perplex, mystify
Conscience: moral sense, principal, scruples, morals, inner voice
Conspire: plot, collude, connive, contrive, hatch, devise, machinate
Contaminate: corrupt, adulterate, pollute, befoul, defile, sully, spoil
Contemplative: introspective, meditative, reflecting, musing, pensive
Contentious: testy, combative, belligerent, disagreeable, antagonistic
Continuity: cohesion, connection, dovetailing, unity, chain, continuum
Contort: disfigure, distort, deform, writhe, bend, convolute, curve
Condundrum: puzzle, enigma, mystery, riddle, quandary
Covet: crave, envy, desire, long for, fancy, aspire to, yearn, lust after
Debacle: catastrophe, collapse, fiasco, quagmire, drubbing, ruination
Debunk: disprove, ridicule, demystify, expose, unshroud, discover
Deduce: understand, infer, glean, gather, conclude, consider, reason
Despondent: depressed, dejected, discouraged, hopeless, forlorn
Desultory: aimless, haphazard, random, rambling, erratic
Diabolical: cruel, fiendish, devilish, heinous, vile, crude, hellish
Discombobulate: confuse, bewilder, mystify, befuddle, nonplussed
Disillusioned: disenchanted, embittered, disappointed, let-down
Dissolute: indulgent, corrupt, depraved, profligate, libertine
Doctrinaire: authoritarian, dogmatic, dictatorial, rigid, inflexible
Dystopia: apocalyptic, fictional, antiutopia, dismal imaginary place
Ecstasy: euphoria, elation, beatitude, bliss, delight, jubilant, fervor
Elixir: panacea, remedy, potion, cure-all, extract, solution, medicine
Emasculate: vitiate, enervate, enfeeble, defenestrate, weaken, dilute
Embellish: exaggerate, hyperbolic, adorn, dress up, enhance, jazz up
Encapsulate: summarize, epitomize, capsulize, synopsize, condense
Encroach: invade, trespass, infringe, usurp, intrude, meddle, entrench
Engorge: gobble, overindulge, pig out, stuff, englut, gulp down, wolf
Ennui: apathy, languor, melancholy, tedium, doldrums, lugubrious
Enthrall: mesmerize, beguile, enchant, bewitch, enrapture, intrigue
Erudite: sagacious, scholarly, cultured, scholastic, highbrow, lettered
Exculpate: absolve, vindicate, pardon, exonerate, acquit, amnesty
Exemplary: ideal, commendable, quintessential, paragon, sterling
Exodus: departure, migration, flight, evacuation, egress, emigration
Extradite: abandon, apprehend, surrender, deliver, bring to trial
Extricate: relieve, disentangle, liberate, disburden, release, remove

Fastidious: meticulous, exacting, finicky, stickler, nit-picky, pedant
Flippant: irreverent, insolent, impudent, frivolous, cheeky, glib
Freewheeling: coast, cruise, drift, sail, skate, float, slide, get by
Frigid: chilly, freezing, Siberian, wintry, cold as balls, arctic, icy
Harangue: diatribe, tirade, spiel, jeremiad, philippic, screed
Hegemony: dominion, authority, command, power, monopoly
Homily: story, fable, sermon, doctrine, lesson, tale, yarn, parable
Humility: modest, self-effacing, unassuming, obliging, self-deprecate
Idiosyncratic: quirky, peculiar, distinctive, oddball, eccentricity
Illicit: illegal, immoral, prohibited, unauthorized, contraband
Illustrious: distinguished, esteemed, eminent, celeb, lofty, exalted
Immortalize: commemorate, canonize, memorialize, praise, deify
Impetuous: impulsive, hasty, abrupt, rash, sudden, restive
Impressionable: susceptible, vulnerable, suggestible, receptive
Inaugurate: commence, initiate, launch, originate, induct, introduce
Indefatigable: resolute, dogged, pertinacious, unwavering, steadfast
Industrious: diligent, persevering, assiduous, productive, laborious
Inept: incompetent, clumsy, inefficient, bungling, maladroit, gauche
Inexorable: inescapable, unrelenting, merciless, adamant, dogged
Infiltrate: permeate, penetrate, pervade, percolate, creep in
Ingenuity: ability, cleverness, resourcefulness, creativity, flair
Inimical: contrary, adverse, opposed, unfavorable, hostile
Insatiable: ravenous, insistent, rapacious, voracious, gluttonous
Intricate: elaborate, tortuous, byzantine, convoluted, complex
Intrinsic: innate, inherent, congenital, natural, deep-seated
Irreconcilable: conflicting, incompatible, incongruous, discordant
Irrevocable: permanent, irreversible, unchangeable, unalterable
Jarring: dissonant, discordant, grating, rasping, clashing, shrill
Jingoism: chauvinsim, fanaticism, nationalism, ethnocentrism
Lethargic: sluggish, sedentary, listless, apathy, dormant, drowsy
Literal: accurate, actual, authentic, to the letter, genuine, true
Lucrative: remunerative, productive, profitable, fruitful, cost
Lurid: gruesome, ghastly, revolting, frim, gory, macabre, obscene
Malevolent: malicious, malignant, wicked, sinister, vengeful, baleful
Malice: animosity, animus, antipathy, rancor, spite, grudge
Mantra: chant, hymn, shout, singing, tune, carol, incantation
Maudlin: mawkish, mushy, sentimental, insipid, weepy, romantic
Menagerie: zoo, aquarium, collection, exhibition, safari park,
Merit: deserve, justify, warrant, earn, incur, get one's due, be worthy
Mythical: allegorical, fabled, fanciful, fictitious, imaginary
Nadir: base, rock bottom, lowest point, floor, record low, zero level

Nefarious: heinous, odious, vile, atrocious, depraved, perfidious
Nepotism: cronyism, favoritism, bias, preferential treatment
Nostalgia: longing, wistfulness, homesick, pining, reminiscence
Notorious: infamous, dishonorable, disreputable, shady, ill-famed
Occlude: prevent, impede, hinder, obstruct, congest, choke, clog
Olfactory: odorous, aromatic, dank, fragrant, malodorous, pungent
Omen: harbinger, indication, portent, premonition, augury, presage
Opiate: narcotic, sedative, tranquilizer, depressant, dope, oxy
Ostensible: alleged, avowed, professed, purported, putative
Partisan: devotee, backer, defender, apologist, disciple, adherent
Platitude: banal, trite, cliché, trope, potboiler, buzzword, hackneyed
Plebeian: commoner, peasant, pleb, plebe, proletarian, rank and file
Plethora: overabundance, deluge, glut, surfeit, surplus, excess
Pollyanna: optimist, fanciful, idealist, glass-half-full, quixotic
Precarious: dangerous, hazardous, dicey, perilous, problematic
Premeditate: think ahead, planned, intentional, intended, deliberate
Pristine: antiseptic, immaculate, sterile, spotless, natural
Probity: integrity, fairness, honesty, rectitude, virtuous, fidelity
Propaganda: disinformation, hype, indoctrination, agitprop
Quid Pro Quo: equal exchange, tit for tat, equivalent, trade-off
Rarified: esoteric, exclusive, select, special, private, elevated, elite
Recluse: hermit, introvert, ascetic, monkish, troglodyte, solitary
Relegate: demote, downgrade, dismiss, displace, eject, exile, banish
Renowned: acclaimed, prominent, notable, illustrious, eminent
Retribution: payback, comeuppance, reckoning, reprisal, vengeance
Reverberate: vibrate, echo, rebound, recoil
Reverie: daydream, fantasy, trance, musing, fool's paradise
Sanctimonious: hypocritical, insincere, self-righteous, smug
Sordid: squalid, sleazy, vile, slovenly, ramshackle, fetid, unkempt
Squelch: stymie, thwart, stifle, squash, repress, muffle, curb, stultify
Staunch: resolute, ardent, stalwart, steadfast, trustworthy, stout
Taciturn: terse, laconic, curt, mum, tight-lipped, silent, withdrawn
Tantalize: provoke, tease, titillate, charm, badger, bedevil, entice
Tawdry: cheap, sleazy, tacky, chintzy, meretricious, gaudy, junky
Tenacious: determined, dogged, stout, fierce, spunky, relentless
Throng: flock, congregation, assemblage, multitude, mob, horde
Totalitarian: dictatorial, autocratic, authoritarian, tyrannical
Tremulous: shaking, palpitating, quavering, shivering, trembling
Unflappable: stoic, impassive, unruffled, nonchalant, inperturbable
Unorthodox: unconventional, abnormal, eccentric, uncustomary
Unparalleled: superlative, exceptional, incomparable, consummate

Unscathed: unharmed, uninjured, in one piece, secure
Unscupulous: immoral, corrupt, unethical, shameless
Vagabond: nomad, trekker, vagrant, itinerant, drifter, roamer
Veneer: pretense, façade, front, gloss, guise, window dressing
Vociferous: loud, vehement, clamorous, obstreperous, uproarious

Attributions

Material Used to create work

Unparalleled: Evan Amos; Free to public
Paragon: Gisele Bundchen show 05; Attribution 2.0 Generic (CC BY 2.0); Luiz Fernando Reis
https://www.flickr.com/photos/7477245@N05/6125344866
Ostracize
Ali https://rigorycriterio.es/articulos/elisabeth-shue-ali-con-i-latina.html
Daniel: https://expressdigest.com/ralph-macchio-and-william-zabka-film-the-karate-kid-reboot/
Resolute: Creative Commons Attribution-Share Alike 3.0 License; CrazyLZ; DeviantArt
https://www.deviantart.com/crazylz/art/naruto-shadow-updated-version-268800545
Encroach
https://dragon-quest.org/wiki/File:DQII_Treeface.png; Square Enix; Tree content is available under Creative Commons Attribution-ShareAlike License
Insatiable: No known copyright restrictions on use; Boston Public Library; File name: 06_10_008792
https://www.flickr.com/photos/boston_public_library
Aerobic: Lance Armstrong
https://time.com/3967661/lance-armstrong-tour-de-france-anniversary/
Pugnacious: Image MGM
https://www.express.co.uk/entertainment/films/977455/Creed-2-who-plays-Drago-actor-Ivan-Drago-son-viktor
Unscathed: Attribution-ShareAlike 2.0 Generic (CC BY-SA 2.0); Roger W
https://www.flickr.com/photos/24736216
Menagerie: Walmart- Creative Commons Attribution-Share Alike 3.0 Unported License; Daniel Case
https://en.m.wikipedia.org/wiki/File:Early_back-to-school_display_at_Walmart,_Kingston,_NY.jpg
Industrious: Free to Use; Mumtahina Rahman
https://www.pexels.com/photo/man-in-a-red-shirt-cycling-a-tri-cycle-3643129/
Encapsulates
https://cavsnation.com/neil-degrasse-tyson-reacts-kyrie-irvings-flat-earth-comment/
Infiltrate: Satoshi Kuribayashi/Minden Pictures
https://www.wired.com/2016/02/absurd-creature-of-the-week-the-huge-bee-decapitating-that-hornet-cant-survive-group-hugs/
Occlude: Upper Respiratory Tract; Blausen.com staff (2014). "Medical gallery of Blausen Medical 2014"; CC BY 3.0; BruceBlaus; WikiJournal of Medicine
https://en.wiktionary.org/wiki/respiratory_tract#/media/File:Blausen_0872_UpperRespiratorySystem.png
Fiasco: School Dance; Creative Commons Attribution 3.0 License; Iris30094
https://www.deviantart.com/iris30094/art/School-Dance-474563217
Prolific: Arnold Schwarzenegger by Namik Amirov; Creative Commons Attribution 3.0 License; 445578gfx
https://www.deviantart.com/445578gfx/art/Arnold-Schwarzenegger-by-namik-amirov-777650792

Illustrious: Babe Ruth; Beer Money and Babe Ruth: Why the Yankees Triumphed During Prohibition; Ben Marks
http://theworldsbestever.com/blog/?s=babe+ruth&x=0&y=0
https://www.collectorsweekly.com/articles/why-the-yankees-triumphed-during-prohibition/
Notorious
Mawe: https://legendsofmen.com/2019/07/why-you-cant-create-a-rite-of-passage-into-manhood/
Contentious: Reuters
https://www.dailymail.co.uk/sport/football/article-1225635/FIFA-reveal-plans-use-jail-trains-hooligans-2010-World-Cup-South-Africa.html
Capitulate: Purple Spector; Creative Commons Attribution 3.0 License; TheDevinciOfOurTime
https://www.deviantart.com/thedevinciofourtime/art/Purple-Spector-695552042
Malevolent: Blogspot
http://fascinationwithfear.blogspot.com/2011/10/halloween-festival-of-lists-october-11.html
http://kazekagames.blogspot.com/2015/06/download-games-jaws-unleashed-fuul.html
Staunch
http://the-thought-that-counts.blogspot.com/2013/03/on-libertarian-lifeguards.html
Hubris: Cosmic Calendar; CC BY-SA 3.0; Efbrazil
https://en.wikipedia.org/wiki/Cosmic_Calendar#/media/File:Cosmic_Calendar.png
Probity: William Penn
https://classroom.synonym.com/effect-did-quakers-beliefs-william-penn-18991.html
Platitude: Grab Life by the Horns; Creative Commons Attribution-Share Alike 3.0 License; goldenmurals
https://www.deviantart.com/goldenmurals/art/Grab-Life-By-The-Horns-368985107
Braggadocio
https://www.mirror.co.uk/sport/other-sports/athletics/brit-ujah-warns-legend-bolt-10908299
Bedlam: d1/rw5jterzxwu.cloudfront.net
https://onedio.co/content/26-memorable-tattoos-from-big-hollywood-movies-10884
Maxim
https://www.machirulos.com/2015/03/orejas-de-coliflor-la-marca-del-guerrero.html
Ennui
https://cdn.hinative.com/attached_images/102232/f4440f2066410f73887a557af6a572279c91258e/large.jpg?1494491718
Inept: Kim Jong-Un Caricature; Attribution 2.0 Generic (CC BY 2.0); DonkeyHotey
https://www.flickr.com/photos/donkeyhotey/36564446304
Unflappable: Jay-Z Zeus; Creative Commons Attribution-Share Alike 3.0 License; zeusphotagraphy
https://www.deviantart.com/zeusphotography/art/Jay-z-zeus-388652318
Pugilist: Wallpaper Safari; You are allowed to use and distribute those as long as you do not remove any copyright or trademark notices.
https://wallpapersafari.com/w/8U49tO
Infallible
http://www.packshotmag.com/films/kfc-presente-le-colonel-sanders/
Personification: Shrek; Fair Use
https://en.wikipedia.org/wiki/Shrek_(character)#/media/File:Shrek_(character).png

Rhetoric: Eminem; Creative Commons Attribution- No Derivative Works 3.0 License; littlekirsti
https://www.deviantart.com/littlekirsti/art/Eminem-403276587
Continuity: Rasta Mouse: Fair Use; File:RastamouseTVtitle.jpg
https://en.wikipedia.org/wiki/Rastamouse#/media/File:RastamouseTVtitle.jpg
Erudite: Elon Musk Royal Society; CC BY-SA 4.0; Duncan.Hull
https://en.wikipedia.org/wiki/Elon_Musk#/media/File:Elon_Musk_Royal_Society.jpg
Extricate: Mega Tsunami in Manchester; Creative Commons Attribution-Share Alike3.0 License; tjblackwell
https://www.deviantart.com/tjblackwell/art/Mega-Tsunami-in-Manchester-136122500\
Keen:
Deadpool Render: Creative Commons Attribution 3.0 License; AlucardNoLife
Deadpool: https://www.deviantart.com/alucardnolife/art/Deadpool-Render-321076152
Wolverine: Wikidot; Creative Commons Attribution-3.0 License
Wolverine: http://marvelrevolution.wikidot.com/logan

*anything used in the frames without a specific attribution comes from and is free to use and modify.

Attributions for material used as reference to create derivative works
Quid Pro Quo
shutterstock - image 116101606
Retribution
Alamy - image BC6XCN
canstock - image 61393750

About AbVocab Publishing, Inc.

Abvocab was co-founded by Matt Quenville and Northeast by Southwest, Inc. in February 2020 to produce, promote and sell Vocabulary based products, including books, interactive websites and general merchandise. In particular, Abocab uses imaginative visuals and usage sentences to engage learners young, old and everyone in between. General Email: info@abvocabpublishing.com

About the Co-Founders

President, Matt Quenville is an educator and entrepreneur. He teaches History at a middle school in Virginia. He currently lives with his wife and 2 children in Hampton Roads, Virginia, where he owns and operates Little Piggy's Wurst Nightmare food trucks and catering. His inspiration for his study book to be soon published was sparked by the lack of engaging vocabulary study guides for the Graduate Record Exam.

Email: M.T.Quenville@abvocabpublishing.com

Vice President, Sketchi Bill, aka Bill Unkel, aka Dr. William C. Unkel has been an educator, scientist/engineer, businessman and the creator of SketchiToons®. Over the years Bill has worked in areas from Plasma Physics to America's Cup technology. His companies have produced science software, unique daylight viewable computer screens and 'Smart Meters.' He currently lives and plays around the city of Santa Fe, New Mexico. Other books by Sketchi Bill are available on Amazon and at www.sketchitoons.com

Email: W.C.Unkel@abvocabpublishing.com

New AbVocab Offering
Sketchi CrossWords™
By Sketchi Bill

Whether you do crosswords or not, the clues and answers of the NY Times crosswords offer a rich selection of interesting words often with a pun or two. The book will include SketchiToons® with words often from the difficult Friday and Saturday puzzles.

Check out the book entries as they appear online and on Facebook. Some will be 'timely' and helpful if you are doing the puzzles.
Fun way to reconnect and to become Absolutely Vocabulous.

Visit: www.abvocab.com/crosswords and @Absolutely Vocabulous on FB

An  Production

Available Now On Amazon
Wait! Wait! I Know That Word!
By Sketchi Bill and Matt Quenville
with SketchiToons® by Sketchi Bill

A humorous and sometimes irreverent picture book where sketches and quips connect you with words to engage family, friends, co-workers, bosses and kids.

Don't be in a Quandary when expressing yourself.

Visit: www.abvocab.com/buy-stuff or On Amazon Look for Sketchi Bill or Matt Quenville

An *Absolutely Vocabulous*™ Production

www.ingramcontent.com/pod-product-compliance
Lightning Source LLC
Chambersburg PA
CBHW040847170426
43201CB00005BB/50